WHERE THE BIG CLUBS PLAY

ABERDEEN
MONTROSE
ARBROATH
BRECHIN
DUNDEE U.
DUNDEE
FORFAR
EAST FIFE
RAITH R.
COWDENBEATH
HEARTS
HIBERNIAN
ST. JOHNSTONE
ALLOA
DUNFERMLINE
STENHOUSEM.
FALKIRK
AIRDRIE
ALBION R.
MOTHERWELL
HAMILTON
STIRLING A.
E. STIRLING
QUEENS PARK
CELTIC
RANGERS
THIRD LANARK
DUMBARTON
MORTON
CLYDE
ST. MIRREN
PARTICK T.
KILMARNOCK
AYR
STRANRAER
QUEEN OF SOUTH
BERWICK
NEWCASTLE
GATESHEAD
SUNDERLAND
HARTLEPOOLS
MIDDLESBROUGH
DARLINGTON
CARLISLE
WORKINGTON

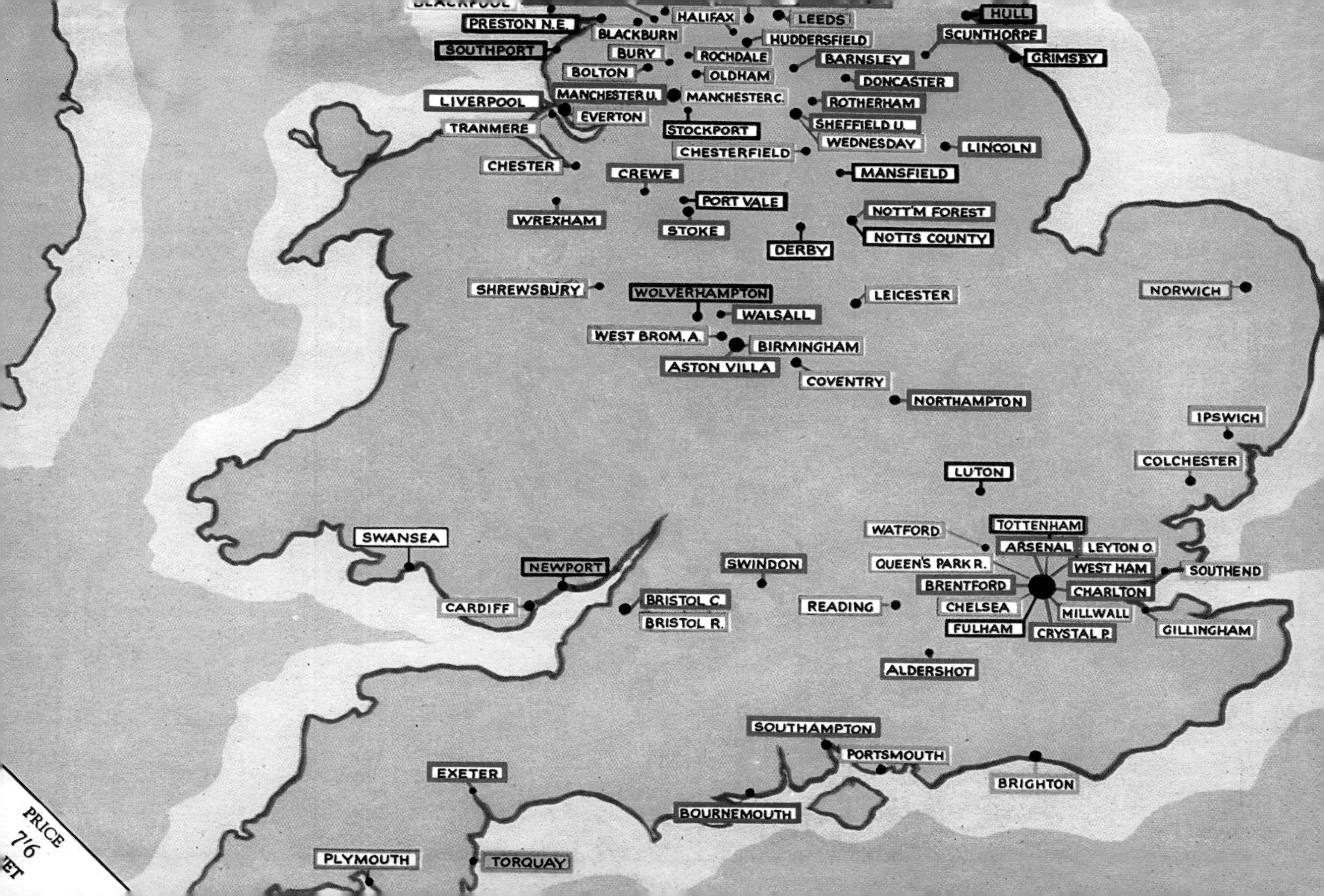
PRESTON N.E.
HALIFAX
LEEDS
HULL
BLACKBURN
HUDDERSFIELD
SCUNTHORPE
SOUTHPORT
BURY
ROCHDALE
BARNSLEY
GRIMSBY
BOLTON
OLDHAM
DONCASTER
MANCHESTER U.
MANCHESTER C.
ROTHERHAM
LIVERPOOL
EVERTON
SHEFFIELD U.
TRANMERE
STOCKPORT
WEDNESDAY
LINCOLN
CHESTERFIELD
CHESTER
CREWE
MANSFIELD
PORT VALE
WREXHAM
NOTT'M FOREST
STOKE
NOTTS COUNTY
DERBY
SHREWSBURY
WOLVERHAMPTON
LEICESTER
NORWICH
WALSALL
WEST BROM. A.
BIRMINGHAM
ASTON VILLA
COVENTRY
NORTHAMPTON
IPSWICH
COLCHESTER
LUTON
TOTTENHAM
WATFORD
ARSENAL
LEYTON O.
SWANSEA
SWINDON
QUEEN'S PARK R.
WEST HAM
SOUTHEND
NEWPORT
BRENTFORD
CHARLTON
BRISTOL C.
READING
CHELSEA
MILLWALL
CARDIFF
BRISTOL R.
FULHAM
CRYSTAL P.
GILLINGHAM
ALDERSHOT
SOUTHAMPTON
PORTSMOUTH
BRIGHTON
EXETER
BOURNEMOUTH
PLYMOUTH
TORQUAY

PRICE
7/6

Frontispiece

Greetings! Roy and the Italian skipper exchange club banners before a match.

THE SECOND BUMPER BOOK OF
ROY OF THE ROVERS

TITAN BOOKS

Titan House,
144 Southwark St,
London, SE1 0UP

Hallo, chums!

Welcome to this year's new *Bumper Book of Roy of the Rovers* which offers a thrilling selection of some of the finest soccer stories, comic strips, features and articles taken from British annuals of the 1950s and 60s in the company of Roy Race, Melchester Rovers F.C.'s top striker and player. I know many thousands of you are already well acquainted with Roy Race, but if you are meeting him here for the first time, then allow me to tell you a little something about him.

Roy is centre-forward and leading goal-scorer for Melchester Rovers, the well-known English First Division League Club whose adventures, both on and off the pitch, first debuted in the British boy's adventure comic *Tiger* in 1954. There he remained until 1976 when he transferred into his own weekly comic, *Roy of the Rovers*, and continued to play until his retirement in 1993.

The Rovers are a grand bunch of lads, playing for a really fine club and I'm sure you'll want to learn more about them. So in this Bumper Book, you'll get to spend a week with Roy and his team-mates, see how a great football club is run and learn a little about the history and folklore of the world's most popular sport. Roy himself will let you in on some of the Rovers' training secrets and, with pictorial tips, offer help and advice to those of you who play soccer on how to improve your game. But rest assured, it's not all work, there are also quizzes and puzzles to test your football knowledge, as well as a splendid joke page.

I hope you'll enjoy meeting Roy Race and Co. And I look forward to talking to you again next year. Cheerio.

Yours sincerely,

THE EDITOR

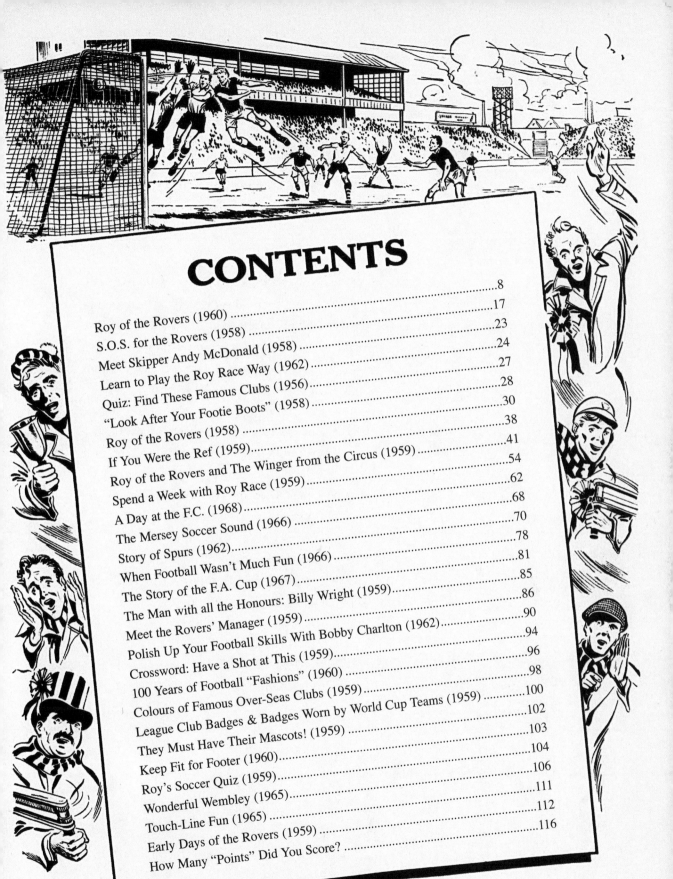

CONTENTS

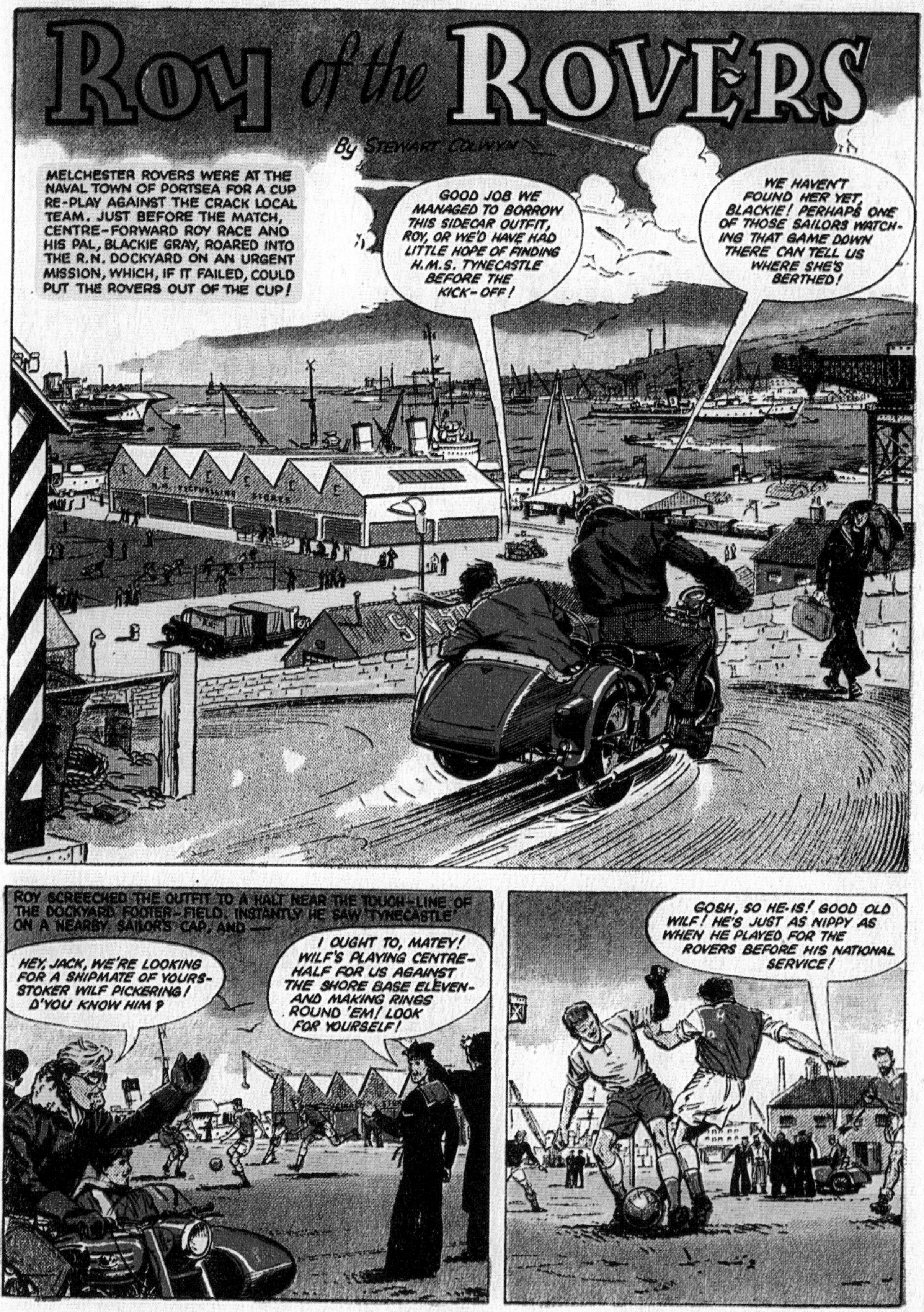
ROY of the ROVERS
By STEWART COLWYN
MELCHESTER ROVERS WERE AT THE NAVAL TOWN OF PORTSEA FOR A CUP RE-PLAY AGAINST THE CRACK LOCAL TEAM. JUST BEFORE THE MATCH, CENTRE-FORWARD ROY RACE AND HIS PAL, BLACKIE GRAY, ROARED INTO THE R.N. DOCKYARD ON AN URGENT MISSION, WHICH, IF IT FAILED, COULD PUT THE ROVERS OUT OF THE CUP!
GOOD JOB WE MANAGED TO BORROW THIS SIDECAR OUTFIT, ROY, OR WE'D HAVE HAD LITTLE HOPE OF FINDING H.M.S. TYNECASTLE BEFORE THE KICK-OFF!
WE HAVEN'T FOUND HER YET, BLACKIE! PERHAPS ONE OF THOSE SAILORS WATCHING THAT GAME DOWN THERE CAN TELL US WHERE SHE'S BERTHED!
ROY SCREECHED THE OUTFIT TO A HALT NEAR THE TOUCH-LINE OF THE DOCKYARD FOOTER-FIELD. INSTANTLY HE SAW 'TYNECASTLE' ON A NEARBY SAILOR'S CAP, AND —
HEY, JACK, WE'RE LOOKING FOR A SHIPMATE OF YOURS-STOKER WILF PICKERING! D'YOU KNOW HIM?
I OUGHT TO, MATEY! WILF'S PLAYING CENTRE-HALF FOR US AGAINST THE SHORE BASE ELEVEN-AND MAKING RINGS ROUND 'EM! LOOK FOR YOURSELF!
GOSH, SO HE IS! GOOD OLD WILF! HE'S JUST AS NIPPY AS WHEN HE PLAYED FOR THE ROVERS BEFORE HIS NATIONAL SERVICE!

AS THE PALS WATCHED, WILF PICKERING STREAKED TOWARDS THE RIVAL GOAL, AND PUSHED THE BALL TO HIS CENTRE-FORWARD, WHO SLAMMED IT PAST THE GOALIE

GOAL! PLAYED, WILF!

UP, TYNECASTLE!

AT LAST THE MATCH ENDED, AND THE PLAYERS TROTTED TO THE TOUCH-LINE

HEY, WILF! OVER HERE — QUICKLY!

THE YOUNG SAILOR LET OUT A WHOOP AS HE SAW HIS OLD ROVERS TEAM-MATES

WELL, BLOW ME DOWN! IT'S ROY AND BLACKIE! WHAT ON EARTH ARE YOU DOING IN PORTSEA-- JOINING THE NAVY?

NO, WILF, THIS IS SERIOUS! LISTEN, TWO OF OUR PLAYERS WERE INJURED IN A CAR ACCIDENT ON THE WAY HERE FOR OUR RE-PLAY AGAINST PORTSEA! WE'VE ONLY ONE RESERVE WITH US AND THERE'S NO TIME TO GET ANOTHER MAN HERE FROM MELCHESTER

BLACKIE TOOK UP THE STORY —

THEN ROY REMEMBERED YOU WERE ON THE TYNE-CASTLE IN PORTSEA HARBOUR, SO MANAGER BEN GALLOWAY SENT US OVER TO SEE IF YOU COULD FILL THE GAP FOR US! CAN YOU DO IT?

GOSH, BLOKES, I— I'D JUMP AT THE CHANCE NORMALLY, BUT IT'S IMPOSSIBLE NOW! YOU SEE, WE'RE SAILING FOR HONG KONG AT 5 O'CLOCK TO-NIGHT!

THUNDERATION, THAT'S TORN IT!

WAIT A TICK! THE MATCH'LL BE OVER BY 4.30, THAT'LL GIVE YOU TIME TO GET BACK ABOARD. CAN'T YOU PERSUADE YOUR SKIPPER?

COME OFF IT, ROY! THIS IS THE NAVY! I CAN'T JUST AMBLE UP AND CHAT WITH THE CAPTAIN! EVEN IF I COULD HE'D REFUSE!

BUT ROY WAS UNDAUNTED

WELL, CAN'T WE COME ABOARD WITH YOU AND EXPLAIN THINGS TO SOMEBODY?

WELL, O.K.! YOU MIGHT GET TO SEE THE COMMANDER, BUT I'M SURE HE WON'T GIVE ME PERMISSION TO PLAY. STILL, COME ON, THE BOAT'S WAITING!

EXCITEDLY, THE PALS JUMPED ABOARD THE MOTOR-CUTTER WITH THE RETURNING FOOTBALL PARTY, AND SOON THEY WERE APPROACHING THE TYNECASTLE

PORT GANGWAY, CUTTER!

IS THAT YOUR COMMANDER HAILING US, WILF?

NO, THAT'S THE OFFICER-OF-THE-WATCH. I CAN'T SEE THE COMMANDER ANYWHERE ON THE QUARTERDECK!

ROY AND BLACKIE FOLLOWED WILF UP THE GANGWAY. THEN, AS THEY STEPPED ON TO THE QUARTERDECK —

WHO THE BLITHERING BLAZES ARE THOSE CIVILIANS? QUARTERMASTER, BRING THEM TO ME—AT THE DOUBLE!!!

AYE AYE, SIR!

CRIKEY, ROY! THAT'S THE COMMANDER!

BEFORE THEY KNEW IT, THE PALS WERE FACE TO FACE WITH THE FIRE-EATING COMMANDER

WHAT D'YOU THINK THIS IS — A PLEASURE STEAMER? WHO IN THUNDER GAVE YOU PERMISSION TO COME ABOARD?

I—I DID, SIR! STOKER PICKERING

IT WASN'T HIS FAULT,—ER—SIR! I PERSUADED HIM TO BRING US

ROY REALISED THAT HE HADN'T CAUGHT THE COMMANDER IN THE BEST OF MOODS FOR GRANTING FAVOURS, BUT HE PLUNGED STRAIGHT INTO EXPLAINING HIS VISIT TO THE TYNECASTLE, HOPING THE COMMANDER WAS A KEEN ENOUGH FOOTBALL FAN TO GIVE WILF SPECIAL LEAVE FOR THE VITAL GAME. BUT THE COMMANDER WAS NOT!

GREAT BLISTERING BILGE-KEELS, MAN, THIS SHIP IS UNDER SAILING ORDERS! NO RATING IS ALLOWED FURTHER SHORE LEAVE—NOT FOR ANY REASON AT ALL!

WITHOUT ANOTHER WORD, THE COMMANDER STALKED OFF, AND WILF SHRUGGED RESIGNEDLY

I TOLD YOU IT'D BE NO GO! SORRY, ROY

IT'S NOT YOUR FAULT, WILF. WELL, WE'D BETTER GET ASHORE AND HURRY BACK TO THE STADIUM! MAYBE THIS MOTOR-BOAT COMING ALONGSIDE'LL TAKE US!

YOU CAN'T GO ASHORE IN THAT, ROY! THAT'S THE OFFICERS' BOAT, BRINGING THE CAPTAIN BACK ABOARD! YOU'LL HAVE TO —

GOSH! SOMETHING'S HAPPENED! THE BOAT'S ENGINE'S CUT OUT!

AHOY, TYNECASTLE! THROW US A LINE, WE'RE IN TROUBLE!

NEXT INSTANT A SEAMAN HEAVED A LINE TOWARDS THE DRIFTING BOAT, BUT IT FELL SHORT!

THE PERISHING WIND'S TOO STRONG! WE'LL HAVE TO USE A ROCKET-LINE TO REACH HER NOW!

ROY HAD A BETTER IDEA. HE GRABBED THE FOOTBALL WILF WAS HOLDING

QUICK, WILF, TIE A SPARE LINE TO THE FOOTBALL LACE WITH ONE OF YOUR FANCY NAVAL KNOTS!

WHAT THE — AH, I GET IT, ROY!

WHEN THE LINE WAS HITCHED ON THE BALL, ROY BOOTED IT AS HARD AS HE COULD TOWARDS THE DRIFTING BOAT

GREAT SCOTT! IT'S A FOOTBALL! UNSEAMANLIKE, BUT MOST EFFECTIVE! SECURE THE LINE, COX'N!

AYE AYE, SIR!

THANKS TO ROY THE BOAT WAS SOON PULLED ALONGSIDE, AND AFTER THE CAPTAIN HAD BEEN PIPED ABOARD, HE TURNED TO THE QUARTERMASTER

GOOD WORK, Q.M.! I WISH TO COMMEND THE RATING WHO USED SUCH INITIATIVE WITH THAT FOOTBALL. WHERE IS HE?

IT WASN'T A NAVAL RATING, SIR, IT WAS THIS VISITOR. HE'S A PROFESSIONAL FOOTBALLER!

IF YOU ASSURE ME THE MATCH WILL END IN AMPLE TIME FOR PICKERING TO RETURN BEFORE WE WEIGH ANCHOR, PERMISSION IS GRANTED! BUT UNDERSTAND, STOKER PICKERING, IF YOU MISS THE SHIP YOU'LL BE COURT-MARTIALLED!

THANK YOU, SIR—I'LL SEE THAT HE'S BACK IN TIME!

THE CAPTAIN WARMLY CONGRATULATED ROY, WHO SUDDENLY SAW A CHANCE TO MAKE ANOTHER EFFORT TO GET WILF ASHORE FOR THE VITAL CUP RE-PLAY. TIME WAS NOW GETTING VERY SHORT, AND HE QUICKLY PUT HIS REQUEST TO THE CAPTAIN, WHO FROWNED THOUGHTFULLY AS HE LISTENED

MORE PRECIOUS MINUTES TICKED BY WHILE WILF CHANGED INTO HIS SHORE-GOING UNIFORM. THEN, AT LAST . . .

COME ON, WILF! WE'VE WASTED ENOUGH TIME ALREADY!

BUT EVEN WHEN WE GET ASHORE YOU'LL HAVE TO BREAK ALL SPEED RECORDS TO GET TO THE GROUND IN TIME, ROY!

AFTER A HECTIC RIDE, THE OUTFIT ROARED INTO PORTSEA STADIUM. THE ROVERS MANAGER, BEN GALLOWAY, RUSHED OUT TO GREET THEM

BY THUNDER, I THOUGHT YOU'D NEVER MAKE IT! GOOD WORK, LADS! GLAD TO SEE YOU, WILF! BUT NOW YOU'LL HAVE TO HURRY, YOU'VE ONLY FIVE MINUTES TO CHANGE!

AYE AYE, GUV'NOR! WE'LL DO IT!

IT WAS A FRANTIC RUSH, BUT WITH ONLY SECONDS TO KICK-OFF, ROY, BLACKIE AND WILF RACED OUT ON TO THE FIELD

COME ON, YOU THREE! UP THE ROVERS!

THAT'S YOUNG WILF PICKERING! HE'S IN FOR A TOUGH TIME!

THE ROVERS WERE WELL AWARE THAT THE CUP RE-PLAY WITH PORTSEA WOULD BE NO WALK-OVER, PARTICULARLY IF McNEIL, THE PORTSEA GOALKEEPER, WAS IN THE SAME TOP FORM AS IN THE FIRST MATCH. IN THAT GAME HE HAD BEEN ALMOST UNBEATABLE THEN AGAIN, THE ROVERS HAD A YOUNG, INEXPERIENCED CENTRE-HALF IN WILF PICKERING, WHO MIGHT FIND DIFFICULTY IN HOLDING THE FAST PORTSEA FORWARDS

BUT WILF QUICKLY SETTLED DOWN AND A FEW MINUTES AFTER THE KICK-OFF, HE SENT ROY AWAY WITH A PERFECT PASS

ROY RACED GOALWARDS AND SLAMMED IN A LIGHTNING DRIVE, BUT . . . .

GOSH! HE'S SAVED IT! IT'S GOING TO BE EVEN TOUGHER THAN IN THE FIRST GAME TO BEAT THAT CHAP McNEIL!

ROY AND BLACKIE RUSHED IN DESPERATELY, BUT THE PORTSEA GOALIE CLEARED WITH A TERRIFIC KICK UPFIELD

THE BALL SAILED HIGH OVER THE CENTRE-LINE, BEAT WILF AS HE ATTEMPTED TO HEAD IT, AND WAS SNAPPED UP BY THE PORTSEA CENTRE-FORWARD, WHO HIT IT FIRST TIME

GOAL! GOOD OLD PORTSEA!

WILF LOOKED GLUM AS HE TROTTED BACK FOR THE RE-START

BLOW ME DOWN! THE PORTSEA GOALIE'S CLEARANCE SCUPPERED ME COMPLETELY! MAYBE I'M RUSTY!

CHEER UP, WILF, YOU'RE DOING FINE! ANYWAY, THE GAME'S ONLY JUST STARTED

FROM THEN ON THE ROVERS ATTACKED ALMOST INCESSANTLY, BUT McNEIL BROUGHT OFF THE MOST MIRACULOUS SAVES

ROY LEAPT HIGH. NEXT MOMENT THE BALL WAS HURTLING STRAIGHT FOR THE NET, BUT —

HALF-TIME CAME WITH PORTSEA STILL ONE-UP. IN THE SECOND HALF THE ROVERS REDOUBLED THEIR EFFORTS, BUT ALWAYS McNEIL STOOD BETWEEN THEM AND THE EQUALISER. NOW THE VALUABLE MINUTES WERE TICKING BY, AND STILL THE ROVERS COULD NOT SCORE. THEN WILF BROKE UP A PORTSEA ATTACK, AND CLEARED TO HIS WINGER, WHO RACED GOALWARDS AND SWUNG OVER A HIGH CENTRE

THAT'S THERE—NO! THUNDERATION! McNEIL'S STOPPED IT!

BUT THE BALL DROPPED BETWEEN MCNEIL AND ROY AS THEY BOTH FELL SPRAWLING. FOR ONCE THE GOALIE WAS OUT OF POSITION, AND ROY SWUNG HIS BOOT ROUND IN A FLASH

GOAL!!

I'VE DONE IT! WE'VE EQUALISED AT LAST!

WILF RAN UP TO CONGRATULATE ROY

GOOD GOAL, ROY! WE'RE ON TERMS! BUT THERE'S ONLY FIVE MINUTES TO GO -- LOOKS LIKE THE GAME'S BOUND TO END AS A DRAW

DON'T WORRY, WILF! WE'LL HAVE TO PLAY EXTRA TIME AND THEN WE'LL WIN! WE'VE GOT TO!

A QUICK LOOK OF DISMAY FLASHED ACROSS WILF'S FACE, AND ROY SUDDENLY REALISED WHY

JEEPERS! I FORGOT-- IF YOU STAY ON FOR EXTRA TIME, YOU'LL MISS YOUR SHIP! YOU'LL HAVE TO LEAVE THE FIELD AT FULL-TIME, WILF, WHETHER WE DRAW OR NOT!

NOT LIKELY, MATEY! I'M NOT LETTING THE ROVERS DOWN NOW! I'M READY TO RISK A COURT-MARTIAL!

THERE WAS NO TIME FOR ROY TO ARGUE. FOLLOWING THE RESTART, BOTH SIDES PUT EVERY-THING THEY HAD INTO THEIR ATTACKS. THEN, WITH FOUR MINUTES TO GO, ROY MADE A DESPERATE SHOT FOR GOAL, BUT —

HECK! MCNEIL'S SAVED AGAIN! WHAT A GOALIE!-

ROY EYED THE GRAND-STAND CLOCK IN DESPAIR ———

WE'VE GOT TO WIN DURING THE NEXT COUPLE OF MINUTES FOR WILF'S SAKE! IF IT GOES INTO EXTRA TIME HE'LL STAY ON AND BE COURT-MARTIALLED, AND I SHALL HAVE TO BREAK MY WORD TO HIS CAPTAIN!

'THEN ROY HIT ON AN IDEA. HE HURRIED OVER TO ROVERS' CENTRE-HALF

LOOK, WILF, YOU MUSTN'T MISS SAILING, AND GET YOURSELF INTO TROUBLE! SO WE'VE GOT TO TRY AND GET THAT WINNING GOAL NOW! SO LISTEN CAREFULLY—

WITH JUST ONE MINUTE TO GO, WILF GOT THE BALL AND FLICKED IT TO BLACKIE, WHO RACED DOWN THE FIELD AND CENTRED TO ROY

McNEIL'S MOVED TO COVER ANY SHOT I MAKE— BUT LET'S HOPE MY PLAN WORKS

ROY FEINTED TO SHOOT FOR GOAL, AND THEN QUICKLY BACK-HEELED THE BALL, KNOWING THAT WILF WOULD BE FOLLOWING UP CLOSE BEHIND HIM

NEXT MOMENT WILF SLAMMED THE BALL HARD AND LOW INTO THE BACK OF THE NET, AND McNEIL HADN'T A HOPE OF STOPPING IT!

GOAL! GOOD OLD SAILOR-BOY!

HE'S DONE IT! WE'VE WON!

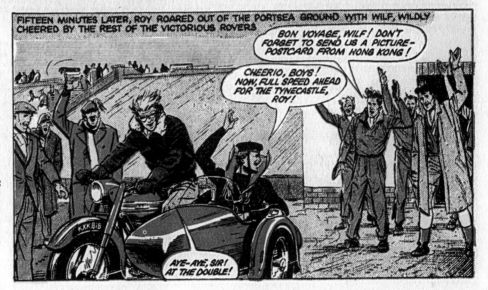

FIFTEEN MINUTES LATER, ROY ROARED OUT OF THE PORTSEA GROUND WITH WILF, WILDLY CHEERED BY THE REST OF THE VICTORIOUS ROVERS

ALMOST BEFORE THE GLUM-FACED GOALIE HAD SCOOPED THE BALL FROM THE NET, THE GAME WAS OVER, AND THE ROVERS' FANS WENT WILD WITH DELIGHT. THANKS TO THE LAST-MINUTE GOAL, MELCHESTER WERE STILL IN THE CUP. BUT WHAT MATTERED EVEN MORE TO ROY WAS THAT WILF PICKERING WOULD NOW BE ABLE TO REACH HIS SHIP IN TIME

BON VOYAGE, WILF! DON'T FORGET TO SEND US A PICTURE-POSTCARD FROM HONG KONG!

CHEERIO, BOYS! NOW, FULL SPEED AHEAD FOR THE TYNECASTLE, ROY!

AYE-AYE, SIR! AT THE DOUBLE!

Carrimore Corgi for Christmas.

Car Transporter · Six Cars with **WHIZZWHEELS**

Gift Set 20
complete 75/-

Presenting the terrific Corgi Tri-Deck Transporter. To be precise
it's a Scammell Handyman Mk III Tractor Unit with
a Carrimore Tri-Deck Mk V Car Transporter.
Ask for Corgi's Gift Set No 20 and get the
transporter together with six powerful sports cars
or you can have the transporter seperately and carry
your own Corgi cars!

Volvo P1800

1146 Transporter
without cars
29/11d.

Lancia Fulvia
Sport Zagato

Pontiac Firebird

Ford Capri
3 litre GT

Marcos 3 litre

MGC GT

All three decks are fully operational and the cab is detachable on this articulated Corgi model.

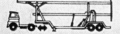   

CORGITOYS

METTOY
PLAYCRAFT

S.O.S. FOR THE ROVERS

Delayed—By a Football!

By Ted Cowan

ROY RACE, centre-forward for Melchester Rovers, pulled up his coat collar about his ears and grinned damply at his inside-right pal, Blackie Gray, as they and the rest of the team hurried across the rain-lashed tarmac of Wendon Airport.

"Sunny Spain, here we come! I can't wait to get out of this weather!" Roy exclaimed.

Rain lashed across the tarmac, reflecting mistily the glow of flare-path and pylons, while ahead of the hurrying Rovers, who splashed water at every step, loomed the four-engined giant which was to fly them to Spain.

"Come on, make it snappy!" yelled burly team manager, Ben Galloway, jamming his soaked trilby down tighter on his head. "The air-liner's waiting!

For Pete's sake, don't let's cause any further delay."

The Rovers were leaving for a short football tour of Spain, and with British weather at its worst, Roy and his pals were not sorry at the prospect of getting away from bleak winds, freak frosts and sleet. For two hours all take-offs had been temporarily suspended, but, at last, the Met Office "o.k." had come through. Now Rovers were on their way to warm sunshine and games on hard grounds.

"Oh, well, the weather is giving us a real old-world send-off, Blackie. Even our airport coach had to break down," Roy added to Blackie.

He broke off, for from behind him somewhere he heard a voice calling his name.

"Roy! Mr. Race! Wait——"

Roy & Co. Stranded at Sea—in a Slowly-Sinking Plane!

Roy turned. Pelting towards him came a youthful airport attendant, his mop of red hair flapping into his eyes. He was clutching a football.

Roy hesitated. The dull bellow of the air-liner's engines, coupled with more frantic yells from Ben Galloway, reminded him that take-off was due very shortly. On the other hand, he felt he could not ignore the wildly running youth.

He waited. At last the uniformed lad reached him, and, panting for breath, thrust the dripping football into his arms.

"It—phew—it's for luck, Roy! From—from Melchester Boys' Club. I work here at the airport, but —but I play for the club. We saved up for this football. Our names are on it!" young Ginger gasped. "Take it as—as a mascot!"

"Thanks, lad! It's a very nice thought," Roy grinned understandingly.

"ROY! For Pete's sake—ROY!" came the sorely tried Ben Galloway's final yell.

Thanking the lad again, Roy ran off.

Holding the wet football to him, he streaked for the white-painted entry stage drawn up by the air-liner—then slipped and fell flat on his face.

"That's right—trying to break your neck before the tour starts!" grunted Blackie, hastily dragging his pal upright.

Watched by smiling officials, Roy was practically bundled by Blackie up the steps and through the air-liner's hatch. They were last aboard. A minute or two later the silvery giant rolled forward, nosed down the runway and swept upwards into the darkness of the night.

"Gosh! A bit of a rush, chaps," Roy exclaimed, unfixing his safety belt. He gazed rather ruefully at his beaming pals, who lounged back in their seats.

His wet coat was off now, revealing his puddle-soaked trousers, which brought forth more banter from his pals. But Roy ignored the grins and passed the mascot ball round.

"I think it was a very nice gesture of these lads," he said.

"Very nice indeed! It's brought you luck already, hasn't it?" half-back Buster Brown chuckled.

Ben Galloway took the ball. But it was still wet and slippery, and promptly slipped from his grasp to go rolling under a passing stewardess's feet.

She tripped. Papers she was carrying went scattering all over Blackie, who nearly had his head jolted off by her elbow. The roar of laughter as Roy hastily recovered his mascot made him wish he had never seen the football.

"Roy, old son, put it away before you kill someone, there's a good chap," Blackie pleaded. "It's a very handsome football, but we've all seen it now, so hide it—and forget it!"

"Nuts!" Roy said impolitely.

He crammed the football into a handy corner by his seat, and did his best to forget all about it. But the good-natured leg-pulling of his pals continued for a long time.

At last things eased off. There was a merry sing-song and then gradual silence. Roy, half dozing, pulled up his travelling blanket and slumped back in his seat.

He smiled as he happened to glance at the football. It was cheap, new and had "To the ROVERS—FOR LUCK!" painted rather untidily in Indian ink above the scrawled names of all its subscribers.

"Good old Ginger!" he murmured, thinking of the excited youngster who had delivered it. "Leg-pulls or no leg-pulls, it'll have a place of honour in our dressing-rooms wherever we go. I'm sure it'll bring us luck!"

Roy dozed off. A few minutes later he was awakened by a queer, jolting movement, which gave him an unpleasant feeling in the stomach. He sat up hurriedly and gazed uneasily around.

Something was wrong. He sensed it in the very movement of the steward, who walked hurriedly past him. Blackie, too, was now sitting up straight.

They released the window blind. Outside the sky was as black as ink still, but the glare of lightning suddenly zipped across it, and played eerily around the rain-gleaming mainplane.

"It's a heck of a storm! Pull the blind down again," Blackie whispered. "Roy, I don't like the look of things. Three times there have been other queer jolts like the one which woke you, and I've seen the steward go into the pilot's cabin."

Another jolt followed. The stewardess in the bar-box spilled three coffees, which simply slid from the tray.

Other players awoke. There were the usual laughs, jokes and wise-cracks—but none seemed quite genuine. That sense of something wrong increased with each minute that passed.

"Perhaps an engine has cut out," Blackie suggested.

"I doubt it," Roy kept his voice low. "Anyway, these kites can fly on three engines without any trouble."

The air-liner lurched sickeningly. All the cabin lights went out for a moment—and then flashed back on.

The stewardess hurried through, and then stopped by each seat.

"There is no cause for alarm, but will all passengers put their safety-belts on," she said calmly and quietly. "It's only a routine precaution."

Roy smiled reassuringly and obeyed without hurry. Yet his face was grim as he turned away after taking a peep out through the blind.

He had seen what nobody else had, at least, none of his team-mates. Silvery objects had flashed past and downwards—and Roy knew that the air-liner had jettisoned her auxiliary petrol tanks.

"Whatever's wrong, it's bad—darned bad! They only do that as a precaution against real disaster," he thought to himself, and glanced again at the football mascot. "I've a feeling we're going to need every single bit of luck that there is!"

Adrift On a Wreck!

ROY said nothing of what he had seen. He joked with Blackie and started a sing-song. Ben Galloway, due to the lurching of the plane, was being violently sick.

"Can I do anything, miss?" Roy asked the stewardess, who again was hurrying back to the pilot's cabin.

She shook her head, and he suddenly noticed she was carrying a first-aid kit. As she closed the hatch after her, a definite puff of smoke drifted out.

"Roy, I can smell carbon tet'—someone's used a fire-extinguisher," Blackie said evenly. "Did you see that smoke? There must have been a fire up front."

"Yes, I noticed it, too! We'd better keep it to ourselves, Blackie," Roy answered. "But I can't understand why we don't climb above the storm."

Another violent tremor of the air-liner stilled Roy's words and flung him forward against the safety-belt's pull.

The forward hatch opened. A set-faced officer emerged, looked around, and walked to midway between the two lines of seats.

"The stewardess is going to issue you with life-saving jackets. I want you all to inflate them—you'll be shown how—and wear them. Next, I'm afraid all heavy luggage will have to be jettisoned. It's all insured. This is an emergency," he announced.

A rather uncomfortable silence greeted his words, and then:

Swiftly Roy and Blackie helped their team-mates to scramble through the window of the crippled plane. It was a desperate battle against time, for with every second the plane was sinking lower in the stormy water!

"May we know what's wrong?" grunted Ben Galloway.

"If I told you, sir, it wouldn't help. But the upshot is we may have to ditch—come down in the sea. But don't be alarmed. That's not necessarily as bad as it sounds," the officer said, and quickly retreated.

"It sounds blooming lovely!" came from some humorist. "Fancy going for a dip at this time of night!"

Despite themselves, everyone chuckled. Then the life-saving jackets were issued, inflated and donned.

Roy let up his blind. Outside, the storm raged and lightning zigzagged. Inky darkness was split again and again by vivid zigzags which tore the heavens in two.

"We're going down, Roy. She's losing altitude," Blackie hissed, checking his harness.

The stewardess and steward moved aft. Heavy baggage whirled from the drop-hatch, seemed to hang in space and then went plummeting downwards.

"All aboard for the Skylark!" Roy murmured to Blackie.

His expression showed nothing of what he was feeling inside him.

"Everyone sit back, please. We're about to ditch," the steward called, and braced himself by the main hatch.

Everyone held tight. There was growing tension —then——

Whooooompf!

A shuddering, jarring shock tore at the fuselage and hurled Roy against his harness. Metal crumpled, and a series of thuds and bangs dwarfed all other sounds.

Roy, as he released his harness and staggered upright, found his nose bleeding. The sound of howling wind and storm-tossed water rose eerily. All lights had gone out in the plane.

"Smash windows and climb out on to the fuselage!" the voice of the aircraft's captain rang through the inter-com.

What followed next was a nightmare. One hatch was jammed, and two crew members injured. But Roy and his team-mates, working under orders, tore out two windows, and then helped each othe outside.

Water beat over them lashed by the wind. But while lightning played above, the Rovers scrambled on to the slippery mainplane and fuselage. Two life-jackets were damaged, and another two had to be left behind, in order that their owners might escape.

The air-liner carried inflatable dinghies, but disaster now followed disaster. One hopelessly jammed in the hatchway, while the other, after its tie-line became frayed through on a sharp metal projection, was carried away by high seas and sank.

Twenty-two people now clung like flies to the crippled air-liner, which kept afloat only by virtue of its great hollow mainplanes and part empty fuel tanks.

At last the wind slackened slightly, and the stranded victims now had a fighting chance.

"We lost radio contact one hour's flying time back," the aircraft's captain told Roy, "but by my calculations we're about three miles off the Spanish coast."

"Surely patrols will come out searching?" Roy said.

"That doesn't mean they'll find us. There's a lot of ocean, and we can't radio our position. The emergency transmitters were in the dinghy we lost," the captain said quietly. "We can only hope that we'll keep afloat until dawn when visibility gets better—but I rather doubt it!"

The prospects were grim. A fast and very treacherous current tugged at the wreck to make things more difficult. The crew fired the only two distress rockets, but no answering light or flare came anywhere from the darkness around.

Not that anyone hoped for much success. In the mist and rain the possibility of the rockets being seen was far from encouraging.

The situation grew worse, and Roy passed his life-saving jacket to one of his team-mates, who could not swim. Then he grabbed the arm of the captain of the plane.

"Supposing I try to swim for the coast, captain. I might be able to make it and give our position," he blurted. "It's worth a try."

"Forget it, Roy, you ass! You'd never make it!" Blackie barked through clenched teeth.

The captain, clinging on beside Roy, shifted his position carefully.

"Your friend's right. The sea's far too bad, and even in a life-saving jacket, you'd soon be a goner. You'd be carried away, perhaps even drowned by the under-tow. No! Our only chance is to hang on here as long as we can and just hope!"

In an effort to revive flagging spirits, Blackie started the Rovers' old footer song. For a moment or so the strains of "Who'd play the Rovers?" battled with the noise of the wind and the furious splashing of the waves.

"Here, what price your lucky mascot now, Roy?" Blackie joked gallantly. "If you ask me, it's a bloomin' hoodoo!"

Blackie's words had a startling effect on Roy.

"The football! Gosh! Yes—the football!" he rapped.

Next moment he had released his grip on the mainplane and went sliding down into the blackness of the waters.

"Roy! Roy!" Blackie called wildly in horror. "Come back, you ass!"

There was no reply. The waters closed over Roy and he vanished from sight!

Nothing To Do But Wait!

BLACKIE'S yell was echoed by others. Incredulity and dismay engulfed the white-faced victims of the air disaster. Each strained his eyes, trying to peer into the depths.

"Blackie, for Pete's sake, what's Roy's idea? What did he say?" Ben Galloway inquired hoarsely. "Surely he's not mad enough to try to swim to the coast?"

"I don't know, guv'nor," Blackie choked. "I'm going down after him——"

"Stay where you are! That's an order!" the captain's voice rasped. "Remember, I'm still in charge here—although your friend seems to think he can do as he likes."

Meanwhile, Roy, his lungs bursting, was coming up under the fuselage. The current sucked and tore at him, but somehow he worked his way along the damaged side.

He was seeking the window he had broken earlier on. It was almost under water, for the fuselage had settled down low.

He rose, gulped in more air, and then submerged again. The next few seconds were a nightmare of endurance and suspense. He grazed his arm on the broken window as he scrambled through it under water.

More seconds sped by. Then his hands found the object he was seeking. It was exactly where he had left it. But now he had to get out with it, and he was almost completely exhausted by the time he broke the surface, and, somehow, reached the great mainplane again.

"Roy!" Blackie cried in relief, suddenly sighting him.

Willing hands dragged Roy to safety once more. Then Blackie and the others stared disbelievingly. For Roy was holding the mascot football.

"Great Scott, are you crazy, Roy? Surely you didn't risk your life to rescue that?" Blackie gasped.

"I did—but for a reason. Has anyone got a tobacco tin?" Roy asked, panting.

"Yes, here's one! Why?" the captain replied.

"Take the lid off it, and scratch our position on it. Make it an SOS. We'll tie it to the football and set

Blackie and the others stared amazed as Roy broke the surface and they rushed to help him out of the water. He had risked his life to rescue a football from the submerged cabin!

it afloat. It may be swept in to shore, or, at least, be picked up by a search craft. It may sound crazy, but it's a chance we've got to take!" Roy said.

The captain saw the sense of what was being suggested. It seemed a slim chance, but he added another idea of his own.

He suddenly dived, as Roy had done, and managed to recover a canister of luminous paint from the emergency kit in the dinghy jammed in the hatchway.

Scrambling back on to the partially submerged fuselage, he daubed luminous paint over the football and the lid of the tobacco tin, on which the message was scratched, giving a "fix" of the floating aircraft's position. Then, with the lid attached to the luminous football, the whole thing was cast adrift and quickly vanished from view in the murk.

"The mist around us here may only be local, and that's why we've not been sighted already. But they're bound to be searching," Roy said, trying to cheer up the bedraggled, gloomy party. "If our luck's in, the current may take the football into a search area, or where the mist's thinner."

"Roy's right," said the captain. "Following our last radio signal before we struck trouble, they're bound to be searching for us. We can only hope the luminous football draws someone's attention."

The storm had died down considerably by now, but the mist thickened and closed in like a heavy blanket.

The situation was decidedly dismal as the wrecked aircraft sank lower. The captain ordered everyone to shift nearer the tail, for trapped air kept this higher above water. But time was running out. One thing was now quite certain, the wreck would never keep afloat until dawn.

"I give it half an hour more," the captain finally whispered grimly to Roy. "After that, it means swimming—but those without life-saving jackets won't last long in this current unless they are particularly strong swimmers."

Roy nodded. He had no life-saving jacket, neither had Blackie.

"I still have hopes of young Ginger's mascot," he thought to himself. "Let's hope it brings us luck this time!"

Silence followed—a grim silence, as the minutes passed slowly. Twice searching aircraft were heard to roar past overhead in the wet mist, but that was all.

No one spoke—it seemed that the last chance of rescue had gone.

Then, with startling suddenness, there came a dull throbbing sound through the murk. It grew steadily louder.

"It's a motor boat of some sort!" cried Roy.

"It's coming this way!" rapped the captain. "Now then, all together—yell!"

They shouted and yelled—again and again in their frantic efforts to attract the boat that was still getting nearer.

Finally, they could make out the glare of a searching spotlight that threw eerie reflections in the mist.

Excitement grew among the half-frozen, sea-soaked party clinging to the wreck.

"Give the Rovers' war-cry, lads!" Roy shouted hoarsely. "Now—all together!"

The Rovers yelled as never before.

At first, it seemed that the motor-launch was moving away from them. The Rovers yelled again, and then——

The light came nearer. All at once an excited hail echoed through the mist.

"Hooray! We've been sighted!" Jim Hallett laughed shakily.

"Gosh! It's like scoring a last minute winner after being three-down at half time!" cried Rovers' skipper, Andy McDonald, in his relief.

A large air-sea rescue launch soon loomed up on them, and in a few minutes all were safely aboard.

Even as the launch turned away the wrecked aircraft sank from view—and with it went all the Rovers' kit! But the players were safe.

Roy, now wrapped in blankets, went up on to the deck of the launch.

"By the way, how did you find us?" he asked an English-speaking Spanish officer. "Was it by chance?"

"Why, no, Senor. It was a football floating on the inshore current! It practically bumped into us," the officer smiled.

"Hear that, Blackie?" Roy chuckled. "Our mascot scored a goal. Who said it wasn't lucky?"

"Roy, you always were a good goal-getter. I hand it to you!" Blackie said fervently.

The whole party were soon safely ashore and enjoying a good meal. Apart from slight shock and exposure, the Rovers were in good trim, while the injured aircrew members were in good hands.

"Roy, I reckon we owe our rescue to you," Manager Ben Galloway exclaimed, when the players were comfortable at their hotel. "If it hadn't been for you——"

"For Ginger's mascot, you mean, guv'nor!" Roy swiftly cut in. "Tell you what, when we get back to England we ought to put on a special match for the Melchester Boys' Club and buy new kit for Ginger and his pals out of the proceeds."

"Hear, hear!" came one mighty chorus.

"But first of all," put in Skipper Andy, "we'll have to think about buying some new kit for ourselves if we're going to play any football out here!"

It wasn't easy playing in new kit, but the Rovers won all three games against Spanish teams—thanks, as Roy said, to Ginger's mascot.

MEET SKIPPER ANDY McDONALD

ROY RACE INTRODUCES YOU TO THE ROVERS' POPULAR CENTRE-HALF

ANDY COMES FROM A SCOTTISH FOOTBALL FAMILY, AND STARTED HIS OWN SOCCER CAREER AS A SMALL BOY. AT THE AGE OF 14, HE PLAYED FOR SCOTLAND IN A SCHOOLS INTERNATIONAL AGAINST ENGLAND. A PROUD DAY FOR ANDY.

WHEN HE LEFT SCHOOL, ANDY FOLLOWED HIS FATHER INTO THE SHIPYARDS AND BECAME A RIVETER. HE KEPT UP HIS FOOTBALL, TOO, WITH A SCOTTISH JUNIOR SIDE. HE WAS A CENTRE-HALF EVEN IN THOSE DAYS.

THEN HE VOLUNTEERED FOR THE NAVY TOWARDS THE END OF THE WAR, AND BECAME A FROGMAN. IT WAS A TOUGH AND DANGEROUS LIFE, BUT ANDY ENJOYED IT.

DURING THIS TIME, HE DIDN'T GET MUCH CHANCE TO PLAY FOOTBALL, BUT HE AND HIS NAVAL PALS KEPT THEMSELVES IN FORM WITH PRACTICE GAMES ON THE FLIGHT DECK OF AN AIRCRAFT CARRIER !

BACK HOME AGAIN, ANDY RETURNED TO HIS OLD JUNIOR SIDE, AND IT WASN'T LONG BEFORE A MELCHESTER ROVERS' SCOUT SPOTTED HIM. THAT'S HOW HE CAME TO JOIN THE ROVERS—AND WHAT A GRAND CENTRE-HALF AND SKIPPER HE HAS BECOME !

ANDY LIVES FOR HIS FOOTBALL, AND IS ONE OF THE FITTEST CHAPS ON THE ROVERS' STAFF. HE PLAYS ALL SORTS OF GAMES WELL, BUT HE HAS ONE OTHER HOBBY—MAKING MODEL AIRCRAFT. HE'S A REAL EXPERT AT IT. GOOD OLD ANDY !

Learn to Play the Roy Race Way

Hallo, pals! Glad to be with you again, so that I can answer some of the playing posers you have sent me. Many of you occupy my own position—centre-forward—and want to know how to deal with a centre-half.

The best way is to give the ball to one of your team-mates and then dash wingwards. The centre-half will have to mark you still, but he'll leave the middle wide open.

Another good move is to bring your wing-half into your attacking scheme. When you receive the ball just outside the penalty area and none of your forwards are near, push the ball behind you. Then dash goalwards, taking the centre-half with you.

The snappy move often brings a quick goal. I recall one we scored recently. I passed to Blackie Gray, who slickly passed it to our centre-half. Our centre-half slammed a long pass to the right winger, who ran in and scored.

If you get into the penalty area with the ball and the goalie's running out, don't just blaze away and miss. Lob it over his head so that it drops into the net.

"Should a defender pass back to his goalie?" Yes, but make sure your goalie knows what you are going to do, and hit the ball hard enough to stop a forward nipping in and poaching a goal.

Always bring the goalie into your attacking schemes. Too many goalies boot the ball hard upfield, sending it only to the opposing defenders, when a pass to a colleague would be far more effective. I like to see one of the wingers drop back to collect such a throw, for while other defenders are engaged in marking the opposing forwards, the winger is often quite unmarked.

All goalies should practise throwing the ball. Over-arm is the best way to get power and direction. Make this part of your training. A few of your pals can stand 30 or 40 yards from your area and you can throw the ball to each of them in turn.

Have you a deputy goalie in your team? A chap who can take over the sweater if your goalie is injured. There should always be one member of a team who could take over between the sticks in an emergency.

Lastly, let me stress upon you all the need for team spirit. Get together once a week and talk over your last match and decide on the tactics for the next one.

Bill learns the hard way

Cigarettes harm your health

FIND THESE FAMOUS CLUBS

Every picture gives a clue to a famous football club. "West Ham" is the answer to puzzle picture one. Try your luck with the rest. Answers, upside-down, bottom right.

1
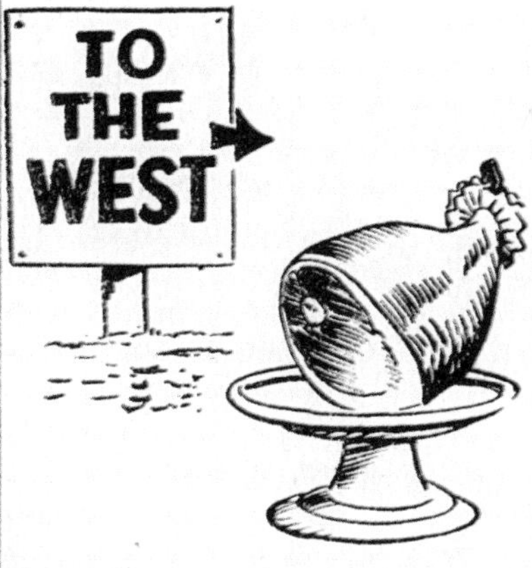
TO THE WEST

2
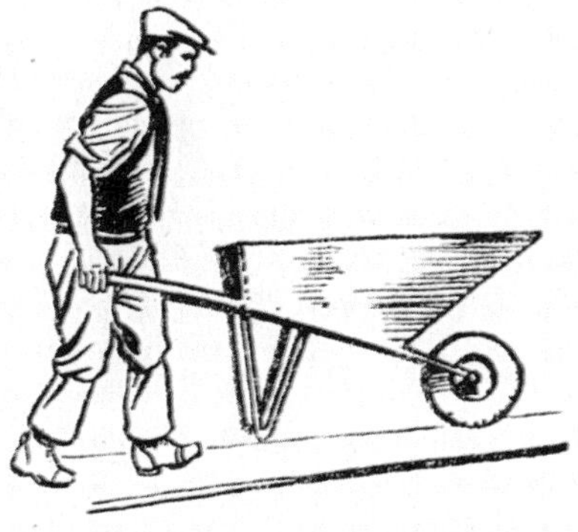

3
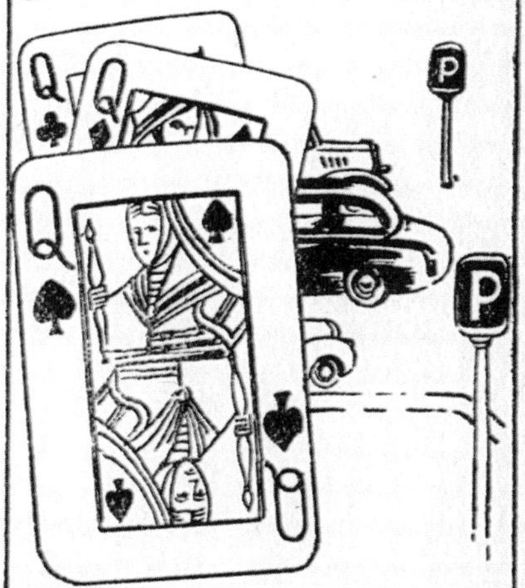
Q
P

4
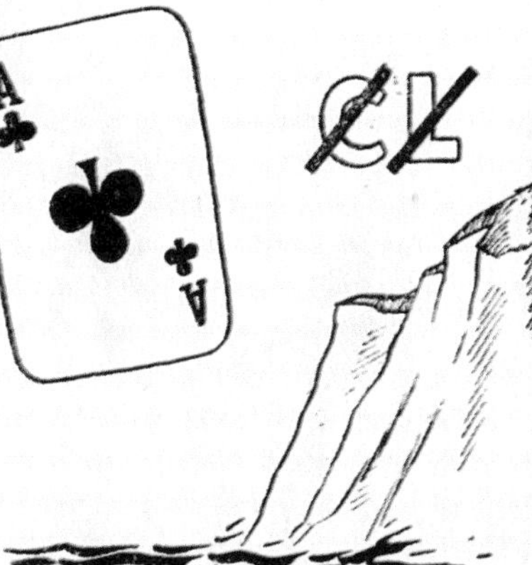
A
CL

5
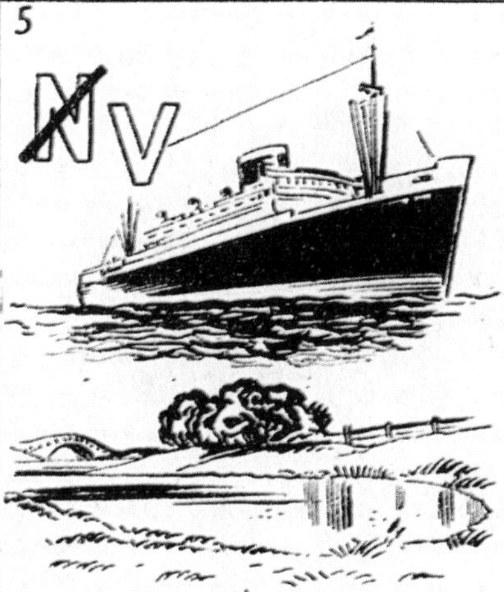
NV

6
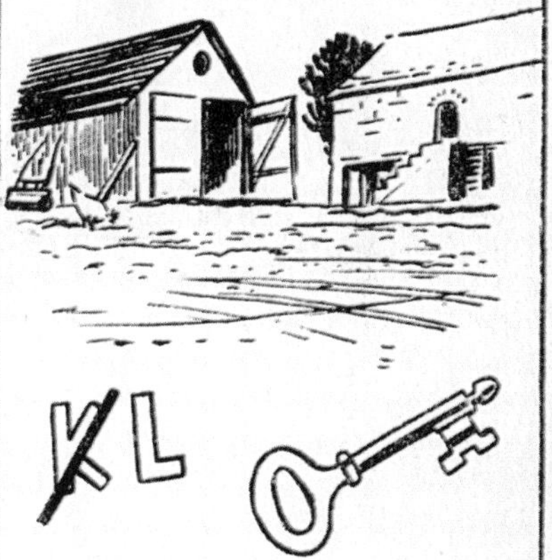
KL

7
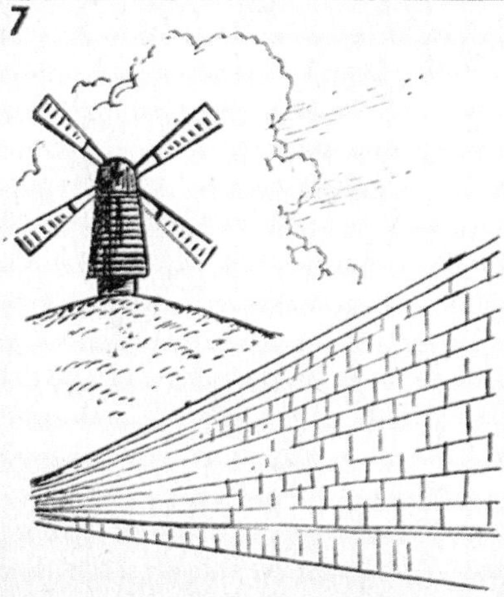

8
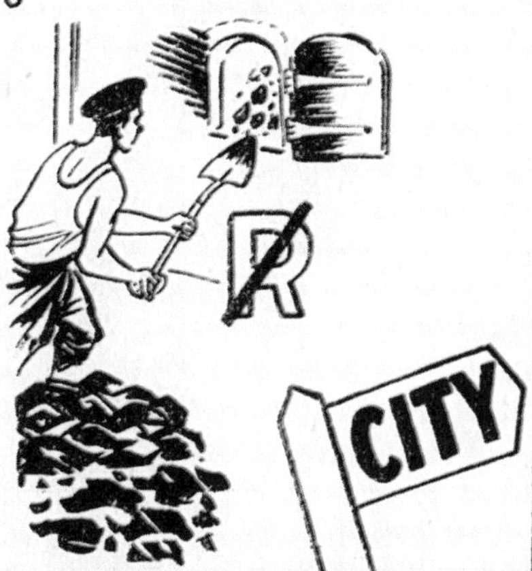
R
CITY

9
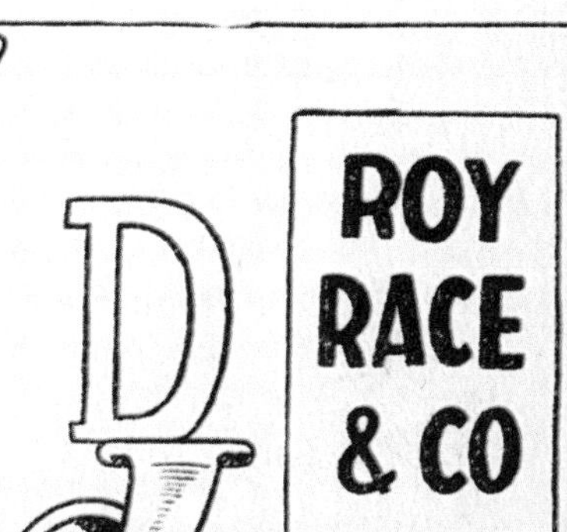
D
ROY RACE & CO

2. Barrow. 3. Queen's Park. 4. Cardiff. 5. Liverpool. 6. Barnsley. 7. Millwall. 8. Stoke City. 9. Doncaster Rovers.

"LOOK AFTER YOUR FOOTER BOOTS"

Says "POP" HONEYWELL, ROVERS' GENIAL COBBLER

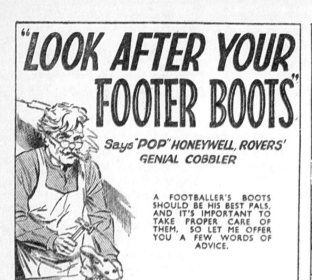

A FOOTBALLER'S BOOTS SHOULD BE HIS BEST PALS, AND IT'S IMPORTANT TO TAKE PROPER CARE OF THEM. SO LET ME OFFER YOU A FEW WORDS OF ADVICE.

THIS IS THE ROVERS' BOOT ROOM, AND YOU'LL SEE THAT EVERYTHING IS KEPT IN FIRST-CLASS CONDITION—INCLUDING THE BOOTS. YOU SHOULD KEEP YOURS THE SAME.

NEVER PUT YOUR BOOTS AWAY DIRTY. AFTER A GAME CLEAN OFF ALL THE MUD, BRUSH THEM THOROUGHLY, AND THEN LEAVE THEM IN A WARM PLACE TO DRY.

BUT *NEVER* DRY YOUR BOOTS TOO CLOSE TO A FIRE! I REMEMBER A YOUNG PLAYER ONCE BRINGING ME A PAIR OF NEARLY NEW BOOTS THAT WERE ALL CRACKED AND SPLIT HE'D RUINED THEM—TRYING TO DRY THEM QUICKLY BY PUTTING THEM ON THAT STOVE THERE!

AFTER PLAYING ON A MUDDY GROUND, GIVE YOUR BOOTS A GOOD COATING OF DUBBIN, LIKE THESE ROVERS' JUNIORS ARE DOING. RUB IT WELL INTO THE LEATHER, BUT NOT ON THE TOE-CAPS. POLISH THESE TO KEEP THEM HARD AND STIFF.

EVERY MEMBER OF THE ROVERS KNOWS HOW IMPORTANT IT IS FOR THE STUDS TO BE RIGHT. SO SEE THAT YOUR BOOTS ARE ALWAYS PROPERLY STUDDED. BY THE WAY, DON'T HAVE YOUR STUDS TOO LONG, OR YOU MAY CRIPPLE YOUR FEET.

WATCHING A JUNIOR MATCH THE OTHER DAY, I SAW ONE OF THE PLAYERS SLIPPING AND SLIDING ABOUT AND MAKING A HASH OF THINGS. THEN I REALISED THAT HE HAD LOST NEARLY ALL THE STUDS FROM HIS BOOTS! FOOLISH LAD!

THERE ARE VARIOUS TYPES OF STUDS—LEATHER, RUBBER, AND THE NEW NYLON SCREW-IN KIND. I SUGGEST YOU STICK TO RUBBER, ALTHOUGH ROY AND CO. PREFER THE SCREW-IN TYPE, BECAUSE THEY ARE EASILY AND QUICKLY REPLACED.

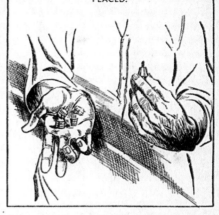

LOOK AFTER YOUR BOOT LACES, TOO. A BROKEN LACE DURING A GAME CAN CAUSE TROUBLE. THE ROVERS FIT NEW LACES TO THEIR BOOTS BEFORE *EVERY* MATCH. THEY DON'T TAKE CHANCES.

CORRECT LACING IS VITALLY IMPORTANT. TAKE THE LACES WELL UNDER THE INSTEP AND ROUND THE ANKLE TWICE, BEFORE TYING THE KNOT EITHER ON THE INSIDE OR AT THE BACK, BUT NOT IN THE FRONT. USE LONG LACES, TOO.

NEVER WEAR NEW BOOTS IN A MATCH UNTIL YOU HAVE BROKEN THEM IN. THE ROVERS USE NEW BOOTS FOR A FEW WEEKS ONLY FOR TRAINING AND PRACTICE UNTIL THEY FEEL ABSOLUTELY COMFORTABLE. YOU CAN EASILY CRIPPLE YOUR FEET IF YOU PLAY A MATCH IN BRAND NEW BOOTS.

ONE LAST POINT. PLEASE DO NOT WEAR YOUR FOOTER BOOTS ON THE WAY TO A MATCH! WALKING ON HARD ROADS OR PAVEMENTS IN STUDDED BOOTS WILL RUIN YOUR FEET—AND WILL DAMAGE YOUR BOOTS. LOOK AFTER YOUR BOOTS, AND THEY'LL BE GOOD PALS!

Roy of the ROVERS

By Stewart Colwyn

CENTRE-FORWARD ROY RACE AND HIS PALS OF MELCHESTER ROVERS WERE AT MELCHESTER AIRPORT. THEY WERE ABOUT TO FLY TO SPAIN FOR A SUMMER TOUR, ON WHICH THEY WERE KEEN TO MEET AND BEAT A NUMBER OF THE BEST SPANISH TEAMS.

ROY TURNED EXCITEDLY TO BLACKIE GRAY AS THE PUBLIC ADDRESS 'SPEAKER BOOMED

ATTENTION PLEASE! WILL PASSENGERS FOR FLIGHT 264 TO SAN REJARRO AND BARCELONA, REPORT FOR CUSTOMS EXAMINATION IMMEDIATELY!

THAT'S US, BLACKIE! SAN REJARRO! IN A FEW HOURS WE'LL BE PLAYING FOOTBALL IN SUNNY SPAIN!

H.M. CUSTOMS AND EXCISE

AT THAT MOMENT, A STRANGER BUTTONHOLED ROVERS LEFT-HALF, BUSTER BROWN

EXCUSE ME, BUT I'M A KEEN ROVERS FAN. SOME PEN FRIENDS OF MINE IN SAN REJARRO WANT ME TO SEND THEM THIS FOOTBALL SIGNED BY ALL THE TEAM. I WONDER IF YOU'D OBLIGE — AND DELIVER THE BALL TOO! THEY'LL BE WAITING AT SAN REJARRO AIRPORT IN A YELLOW AJAX CAR.

WELL — I — I SUPPOSE SO! HEY, CHAPS, HOLD ON A MINUTE!

ROY AND CO. WERE DELIGHTED TO SIGN THEIR NAMES ON THE SOUVENIR FOOTBALL

THANKS A LOT, ROVERS! IT'LL GIVE MY SPANISH FRIENDS A BIG KICK TO HAVE THE BALL PRESENTED IN PERSON BY ONE OF YOU

NO TROUBLE AT ALL! WE'LL MAKE SURE IT GETS TO THEM O. K.

SOON THE ROVERS PLANE WAS WINGING SOUTHWARDS FOR SPAIN AND SAN REJARRO

BETTER TAKE IT EASY WHILE WE'VE GOT THE CHANCE, LADS! WE'RE GOING TO HAVE A HARD GAME AGAINST SAN REJARRO

YOU'RE RIGHT, ROY! WE'VE GOT TO BE ON TOP FORM TO BEAT 'EM. THEY HAVEN'T LOST TO A BRITISH TEAM SO FAR AND WE WANT TO BE THE FIRST TO BREAK THEIR RECORD!

SEVERAL HOURS LATER, THEY TOUCHED DOWN ON SAN REJARRO'S SUN-BAKED AIRFIELD

COME ON, BOYS THE SOONER WE GET THROUGH CUSTOMS THE QUICKER WE CAN COOL OFF AT OUR HOTEL!

WE'LL NEED TO! IT'LL BE HOT ENOUGH TO FRY EGGS ON THE SOCCER PITCH THIS AFTERNOON!

WELCOME TO SAN REJARRO, SENORS! ZIS WAY TO ZE CUSTOMS PLEASE!

A CUSTOMS OFFICER NODDED TO THE BALL BUSTER WAS DELIVERING . . .

I SEE YOU BRING YOUR OWN FOOTBALL WIZ YOU, SENOR! BUT WHAT IS ZE WRITING ON IT?

IT'S ONLY A SOUVENIR FOOTBALL WITH ALL OUR SIGNATURES ON IT. I'M DELIVERING IT FOR A FRIEND

AH, I SEE! GRACIAS, SENOR, YOU MAY TAKE IT THROUGH

OUTSIDE THE CUSTOMS BUILDING —

WELL, THAT WASN'T MUCH TROUBLE, ROY! NOW WHERE'S THIS YELLOW CAR I'M SUPPOSED TO LOOK FOR?

THAT MUST BE IT—LOOK! THEY'RE WAVING! HURRY UP AND HAND THE BALL OVER TO THEM, BUSTER, WE'VE GOT TO BE ON OUR WAY

BUT AT THAT MOMENT, ONE OF THE CUSTOMS MEN WAS ANSWERING AN URGENT TELEPHONE CALL IN HIS OFFICE, AND . . . .

ZUT! WE MUST ACT AT ONCE! QUICK, GONZALES! OUTSIDE! ARREST ZAT INGLEE'S FOOTBALLER — ZE ONE CARRYING ZE BALL!

MEANWHILE, BUSTER HAD JUST REACHED THE YELLOW CAR

HALT! STAND WHERE YOU ARE!

WHAT THE — —?

CARAMBA! ZE CUSTOMS MUST HAVE BEEN WARNED! QUICK, CARLOS, GRAB ZE FOOTBALL. ZEY MUST NOT GET IT

REALISING THE CUSTOMS MEN WANTED THE BALL, BUSTER HUNG ON TO IT BUT NEXT INSTANT HE WAS DRAGGED INTO THE CAR AS IT SHOT AWAY

STOP! STOP OR I FIRE!

HEY! DON'T SHOOT! THERE'S ONE OF OUR PALS IN THAT CAR!

WE 'AVE JUST BEEN WARNED BY AN AGENT IN BRITAIN ZAT ZE FOOTBALL YOUR FRIEND WAS DELIVERING CONTAINED CONTRABAND DIAMONDS! HE WILL FACE A SERIOUS CHARGE OF SMUGGLING!

BUT THAT'S RIDICULOUS! BUSTER DIDN'T KNOW ANYTHING ABOUT IT. HE THOUGHT HE WAS JUST DOING A SOCCER FAN A FAVOUR——

BUT THE OFFICER IMPATIENTLY PUSHED ROY ASIDE---

ZERE IS NO TIME TO ARGUE! GONZALES--TAKE TWO MEN AND FOLLOW ZAT CAR! ZEY MUST NOT GET AWAY! SHOOT IF NECESSARY!

SI, SI, SENOR! PRONTO!

ROY GASPED IN DISMAY, AS A JEEP ROARED OFF IN PURSUIT

GOOD GOSH, BLACKIE! BUSTER'S IN GREAT DANGER! EVEN IF THOSE SMUGGLERS DON'T BUMP HIM OFF, THE CUSTOMS MEN MIGHT ARREST HIM! AND WE'VE GOT TO GET HIM BACK TO PLAY IN THE MATCH!

WAIT! WHO'S THIS CHAP?

HEY, YOU GUYS, I SAW AND HEARD WHAT HAPPENED! JUMP ABOARD MY HELICOPTER-- WE'LL GO AFTER 'EM!

WITHOUT WASTING TIME, ROY AND BLACKIE LEAPT ABOARD THE HELPFUL AMERICAN'S HOVER-PLANE AND TOOK OFF AT ONCE

DON'T LOOK SO SURPRISED! I'M CHUCK BRADY, SEA RESCUE 'COPTER PILOT! MY JOB IS TO PATROL THE LOCAL BEACHES AND LOOK OUT FOR ANY SWIMMERS IN DISTRESS

GOSH! WELL, THANKS FOR YOUR HELP--I HOPE YOU CAN RESCUE OUR PAL, EVEN THOUGH HE ISN'T SWIMMING!

THE 'COPTER THRASHED ALONG HIGH ABOVE THE ROAD WHICH THE SMUGGLERS HAD TAKEN THEN

THERE'S THE YELLOW CAR! IT'S TURNED INLAND-- TOWARDS THE MOUNTAINS!

YEAH! AND THEY'VE GIVEN THE CUSTOMS GUYS THE SLIP! LOOK--- THE JEEP'S GONE STRAIGHT ON!

FAR BELOW, THE SMUGGLERS HAD REACHED A CABLE-HOIST ACROSS A GAPING RAVINE

ALL RIGHT, INGLEES-- INTO ZE CABLE-CAR, AND PLAY NO TRICKS, OR YOU WEEL REGRET IT!

YOU DIRTY CROOKS! I DON'T KNOW WHAT YOUR GAME IS, BUT YOU WON'T GET AWAY WITH IT!

WHO WILL STOP US? ONCE ACROSS ZE RAVINE, WE WILL DISAPPEAR INTO ZE HIGH SIERRAS! AS FOR YOU, AMIGO, YOU WILL NOT LIVE TO TELL ANYONE--

SE PROHIBI

NEXT MINUTE THE CABLE-CAR SWUNG OUT OVER THE DIZZY CHASM. THEN SUDDENLY...

MIGUEL! LOOK--A HELICOPTER!

CARAMBA! IT IS FOLLOWING US! SHOOT AT IT, CARLOS-- SHOOT!

THE CROOKS FORGOT BUSTER, AS THEY TOOK AIM AT THE SWOOPING 'COPTER, UNTIL--

LOOK OUT, CHUCK! THEY'RE SHOOTING AT US!

OH, NO YOU DON'T!

THE CABLE-CAR SWUNG CRAZILY IN SPACE WHILE BUSTER STRUGGLED DESPERATELY WITH HIS CAPTORS

ABOARD THE 'COPTER, ROY GASPED WITH HORROR

BY THUNDER! THEY'RE GETTING THE BETTER OF BUSTER! THEY MEAN TO PUSH HIM OUT! QUICK, BLACKIE, INTO THE RESCUE NET! CHUCK-- LOWER US IN THE NET AS QUICKLY AS YOU CAN!

JUST AS IT SEEMED NOTHING COULD SAVE BUSTER FROM HURTLING INTO SPACE--

GOT YOU!

AGH!

ROY! BLACKIE! THANK THE STARS!

CARLOS RAISED HIS AUTOMATIC WITH A SNARL OF FURY, BUT:...

WELL DONE, BLACKIE!

BEFORE THE SMUGGLERS COULD RECOVER, BUSTER WHIPPED UP THE FALLEN GUN, AND....

O.K., I'VE GOT 'EM COVERED! GOSH, AM I GLAD TO SEE YOU CHAPS! HEY, ROY! ARE YOU ALL RIGHT?

ROY WAS WINCING WITH PAIN AS HE SCRAMBLED GROGGILY TO HIS FEET

I THINK SO, BUSTER. JUST BASHED MY KNEE AS I LANDED, AND IT GAVE ME GYP FOR A BIT! NOW LET'S GET THESE JOKERS TO THE POLICE, AND THEN WE'VE GOT TO GET BACK TO SAN REJARRO IN TIME FOR THE MATCH

AT THE POINT OF THEIR OWN GUN, THE CROOKS WERE FORCED INTO THE RESCUE NET. THEN CHUCK LOWERED A ROPE LADDER FOR THE PALS TO CLIMB ABOARD THE HOVER-PLANE

SMART WORK, BOYS! WE'LL LEAVE THOSE GUYS HANGING IN THE NET

RIGHT, CHUCK! THE SOONER WE HAND THEM AND THE STUFF THEY WERE SMUGGLING OVER THE BETTER! THEN WE MUST GET BACK TO SAN REJARRO AT THE DOUBLE! THE ROVERS WILL BE WORRIED STIFF!

ONCE ROY, BLACKIE AND BUSTER WERE SAFELY ABOARD THE PLANE, CHUCK OPENED THE THROTTLE AND THEY SOARED UP OVER THE MOUNTAINS AT TOP SPEED, WITH THE TWO TERRIFIED CROOKS DANGLING BELOW LIKE NETTED FISH! DURING THE FLIGHT, ROY CUT OPEN THE SOUVENIR FOOTBALL AND, SURE ENOUGH, FOUND A LARGE PACKET OF DIAMONDS HIDDEN BETWEEN THE BLADDER AND THE CASING! BY SMUGGLING THE GEMS, THE CROOKS WERE TRYING TO CHEAT THE CUSTOMS OUT OF THOUSANDS OF POUNDS DUTY.

BUT AFTER A WHILE, CHUCK HAD TO LAND AT A CIVIL GUARD POST SOME MILES OUT OF SAN REJARRO BECAUSE HE WAS SHORT OF PETROL. THERE, THE PALS EXPLAINED EVERYTHING TO THE STARTLED COMMANDANT

MAGNIFICO! IF WHAT YOU SAY IS TRUE, SENOR, YOU 'AVE BROKEN A SMUGGLING RING ZE AUTHORITIES 'AVE BEEN TRYING TO CATCH FOR MONTHS!

WELL, WOULD YOU TELEPHONE THE CUSTOMS OFFICER AT SAN REJARRO AIRFIELD? HE'LL CONFIRM WHAT HAPPENED -- AND I HOPE HE'LL CLEAR BUSTER BROWN HERE OF BEING INVOLVED

THE COMMANDANT DISAPPEARED INTO THE POST. MINUTES TICKED BY, AND ROY BEGAN TO LOOK ANXIOUSLY AT HIS WATCH. THEN AT LAST...

BUENO, SENORS! I 'AVE CONTACT ZE CUSTOMS OFFICER, AND HE SEND HIS GRATITUDE AND APOLOGIES TO SENOR BROWN FOR HAVING ACCUSED HIM. YOU ARE FREE TO GO!

THAT'S A RELIEF! BUT OUR HELICOPTER'S OUT OF PETROL--- AND WE'VE GOT TO GET BACK TO SAN REJARRO IN TIME FOR THE MATCH! COULD YOU FIX US SOME TRANSPORT?

THE COMMANDANT OBLIGED, AND WITHIN SECONDS, THE PALS WERE ROARING OFF IN A JEEP

ADIOS SENORS-- AND GOOD LUCK!

SO LONG, FELLERS! I'LL TRY AND GET THERE IN TIME TO SEE YOU TAN THE PANTS OFF SAN REJARRO!

CHEERIO-- AND THANKS!

MEANWHILE, AT SAN REJARRO STADIUM, MANAGER BEN GALLOWAY DASHED INTO THE ROVERS' DRESSING-ROOM

GREAT NEWS, LADS! I'VE JUST HAD A PHONE CALL. ROY AND BLACKIE HAVE RESCUED BUSTER! THEY'RE ALL O.K., AND ON THEIR WAY HERE!

THANK THE STARS FOR THAT! BUT I HOPE THEY GET HERE BEFORE KICK-OFF! WE CAN'T AFFORD TO START WITHOUT 'EM AGAINST A TEAM LIKE SAN REJARRO!

IT'S NEARLY TIME, LADS. YOU'LL HAVE TO GO ON WITHOUT 'EM, AND —

DUCHA

HI, ROVERS! WE'RE HERE!

HOORAY! THEY MADE IT!

THANK HEAVEN YOU'RE SAFE, BOYS! GET CHANGED QUICKLY, THEN GO OUT THERE AND GIVE SAN REJARRO A GAME THEY'LL REMEMBER!

TEN MINUTES LATER, THE ROVERS BEGAN TO GIVE THE SPANISH CROWD A FINE DISPLAY OF FOOTBALL AS THEY SWEPT INTO ATTACK AFTER ATTACK. THEN BLACKIE RACED ON TO A PASS FROM PADDY —

HE SWERVED NIMBLY ROUND A PLUNGING BACK AND SWUNG A PERFECT CENTRE TO ROY

ROY TOOK THE PASS, BUT SEEMED TO STUMBLE! THEN, JUST BEFORE A CHARGING SPANIARD SENT HIM SPRAWLING —

CARAMBA! ZE INGLEES ARE WIZARDS!

GOAL! OLÉ!

OLÉ!!

BUT THE ROVERS' JUBILATION WAS CUT SHORT AS THEY SAW ROY STAGGERING TO HIS FEET, OBVIOUSLY IN PAIN

YOU TOOK A BAD SPILL, ROY! ARE YOU O.K.?

PHEW! THAT KNEE I BASHED ON THE CABLE-HOIST GAVE ME A BAD TWINGE! BUT DON'T WORRY—I CAN CARRY ON! I—I'VE GOT TO!

BUT IT SOON BECAME OBVIOUS THAT ROY WAS NOT IN VERY GOOD SHAPE

YOURS, ROY!

MISSED IT! THIS PERISHING KNEE LET ME DOWN!

A SHORT TIME LATER, SAN REJARRO SWEPT THROUGH AND SLAMMED HOME A SPECTACULAR EQUALISER!

GOAL!

BRAVO SAN REJARRO! MUY BUENO!

AFTER THAT, THE ROVERS WERE FORCED TO PLAY THE DEFENSIVE. ROY WAS VIRTUALLY A PASSENGER, AND BUSTER, SHAKEN BY HIS EXPERIENCE, WAS ALSO BADLY OFF FORM. ONLY THE MIRACULOUS SAVES OF GOALIE LEN DOLLAND STOPPED THE SCORE PILING UP AGAINST THEM

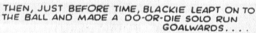

THEN, JUST BEFORE TIME, BLACKIE LEAPT ON TO THE BALL AND MADE A DO-OR-DIE SOLO RUN GOALWARDS....

DESPITE THE RUGGED SPANISH DEFENCE, BLACKIE FORCED HIS WAY THROUGH TO THE GOAL AREA AND SHOT, BUT...

DARN IT! HIT THE POST!

BUT ROY SAW THE BALL CURLING BACK TOWARDS HIM . . .

I'VE GOT TO BEAT THAT BACK TO IT! IF ONLY MY KNEE WILL HOLD OUT!

ROY MADE ONE LAST DESPERATE EFFORT, AND . . .

GOAL! PLAYED, ROY!

AT THAT MOMENT THE FINAL WHISTLE BLEW, AND THE ROVERS WENT WILD WITH EXCITEMENT!

WE'VE DONE IT! WE'VE BEATEN SAN REJARRO 2-1!

AND IT'S THANKS TO GOOD OLD ROY — BY GOSH, LOOK! ROY'S STILL ON THE GROUND HE'S OUT FOR THE COUNT!

FOLLOWED BY THE ANXIOUS TEAM, BLACKIE AND BUSTER BROWN CARRIED ROY INTO THE DRESSING ROOM, WHERE ROY CAME TO . . .

WH-WHERE AM I? WHAT HAPPENED?

YOU SCORED THE WINNING GOAL, THAT'S WHAT HAPPENED, OLD SPORT — BUT HOW'S THAT KNEE, TAFF?

IT'LL BE AS GOOD AS NEW IN A COUPLE OF DAYS. COULD'VE BEEN A LOT WORSE!

GOSH! I CAN'T EVEN REMEMBER SCORING THAT LAST GOAL — I MUST'VE BLACKED OUT WITH THE PAIN JUST AS I REACHED THE BALL! BUT WE WON AND THAT'S ALL THAT MATTERS!

LATER THAT EVENING . . .

WELL, LADS, THANKS TO ROY AND BLACKIE'S TIMELY RESCUE OF BUSTER, WE'VE STARTED OUR SPANISH TOUR WITH A BANG!

HEAR, HEAR, GUV'NOR!

HERE'S HOPING THE REST OF THE TOUR'S AS SUCCESSFUL!

THE END

IF YOU WERE THE REF

WHAT DECISIONS WOULD **YOU** GIVE IN THE FOLLOWING INCIDENTS IF YOU WERE THE MAN WITH THE WHISTLE? (Correct decisions are given on page 158.)

THE GOALIE JUST MANAGED TO TOUCH A SHOT, BUT THE BALL ROLLED ALONG THE LINE, HIT THE INSIDE OF THE FAR POST, AND BOUNCED OUT. WOULD YOU AWARD A GOAL?

AS A PLAYER PICKS UP THE BALL FOR A THROW-IN, ONE OF THE MEN MOVING ACROSS TOWARDS THE TOUCHLINE FOULS AN OPPONENT. WHAT KIND OF FREE-KICK WOULD YOU GIVE?

YOU TAKE THE FIELD WITH YOUR LINESMEN FOR AN IMPORTANT MATCH AND SEE THERE ARE NO FLAGS MARKING THE HALFWAY LINE. WHAT SHOULD YOU DO?

A FORWARD WAS CHALLENGING THE GOALIE, SO THE GOALIE PUSHED HIM OUT OF THE WAY WITH THE BALL, AND THEN CLEARED. WOULD YOU ALLOW THIS?

DURING A MATCH THE CROSSBAR OF ONE OF THE GOALS WAS DISPLACED AND CRACKED. THERE WAS NO OTHER CROSSBAR AVAILABLE, SO THE REF. ORDERED A PIECE OF ROPE TO BE STRETCHED BETWEEN THE POSTS. WAS HE RIGHT?

A FORWARD TOOK A SHOT AND THE BALL STRUCK THE CROSSBAR. IT BOUNCED OUT AND HIT A FULL-BACK ON THE ARM, ALTHOUGH HE WAS NOT LOOKING AT THE BALL. WOULD YOU AWARD A PENALTY?

CENTRE-FORWARD (LEFT) SLIPPED THE BALL PAST THE FULL-BACK, AND HIS INSIDE-RIGHT (8) DASHED FORWARD, PICKED UP THE PASS, AND SLAMMED IT INTO THE GOAL. THE REFEREE DISALLOWED THE GOAL BECAUSE HE SAID THE INSIDE-RIGHT WAS OFFSIDE. DO YOU AGREE?

A PLAYER MISSED A PENALTY KICK, BUT THE REF. ORDERED THE KICK TO BE RETAKEN, AND ANOTHER PLAYER STEPPED UP TO TAKE IT. WOULD YOU ALLOW THIS, OR ORDER THE FIRST PLAYER TO RETAKE THE SPOT-KICK?

ONE TEAM PLAYED WITH ONLY 10 MEN UNTIL HALF-TIME. THEN, AS SOON AS THE SECOND HALF STARTED, THEIR MISSING PLAYER TURNED UP. WOULD YOU ALLOW HIM TO TAKE THE FIELD AND PLAY?

THE LAWS STATE THAT ALL PLAYERS MUST STAND 10 YARDS FROM THE BALL WHEN A FREE-KICK IS TAKEN, BUT IN THIS CASE, WHEN AN INDIRECT FREE-KICK WAS AWARDED IN THE GOAL AREA, SOME OF THE DEFENDING SIDE TOOK UP POSITION **ON** THE GOAL-LINE, ONLY A FEW YARDS FROM THE BALL. WOULD YOU ALLOW THE KICK TO BE TAKEN?

A FAIR SHOULDER CHARGE IS PERMISSIBLE, BUT WOULD YOU ALLOW THIS ONE TO PASS WITHOUT PENALTY? LOOK AT IT CLOSELY BEFORE YOU DECIDE.

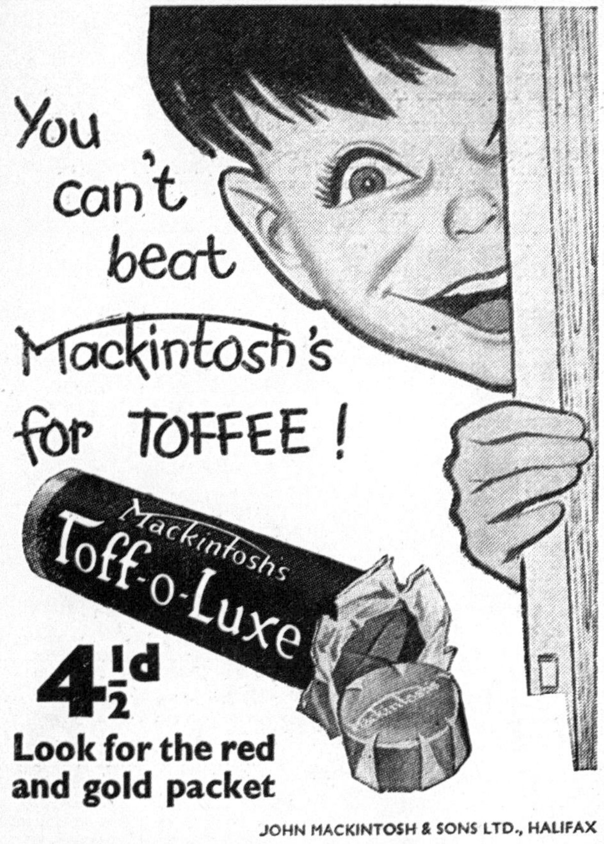
You can't beat Mackintosh's for TOFFEE!
Mackintosh's Toff-o-Luxe
4½d
Look for the red and gold packet
JOHN MACKINTOSH & SONS LTD., HALIFAX

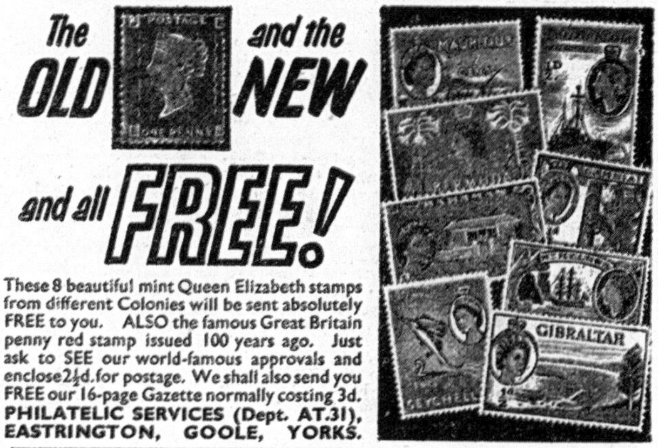
The OLD and the NEW and all FREE!
These 8 beautiful mint Queen Elizabeth stamps from different Colonies will be sent absolutely FREE to you. ALSO the famous Great Britain penny red stamp issued 100 years ago. Just ask to SEE our world-famous approvals and enclose 2½d. for postage. We shall also send you FREE our 16-page Gazette normally costing 3d.
PHILATELIC SERVICES (Dept. AT.31), EASTRINGTON, GOOLE, YORKS.

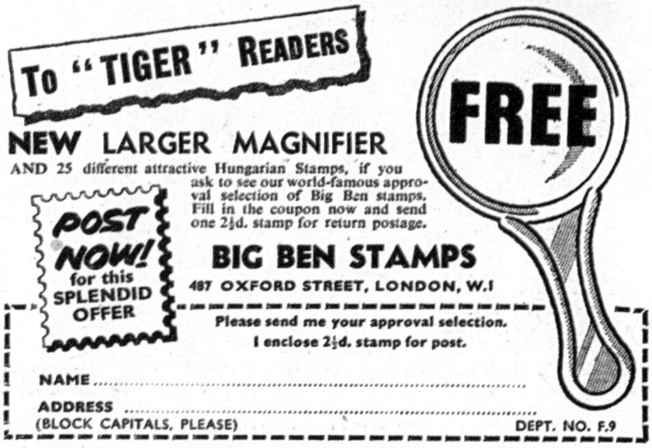
To "TIGER" READERS
FREE
NEW LARGER MAGNIFIER
AND 25 different attractive Hungarian Stamps, if you ask to see our world-famous approval selection of Big Ben stamps. Fill in the coupon now and send one 2½d. stamp for return postage.
POST NOW! for this SPLENDID OFFER
BIG BEN STAMPS
487 OXFORD STREET, LONDON, W.1
Please send me your approval selection.
I enclose 2½d. stamp for post.
NAME
ADDRESS
(BLOCK CAPITALS, PLEASE)
DEPT. NO. F.9

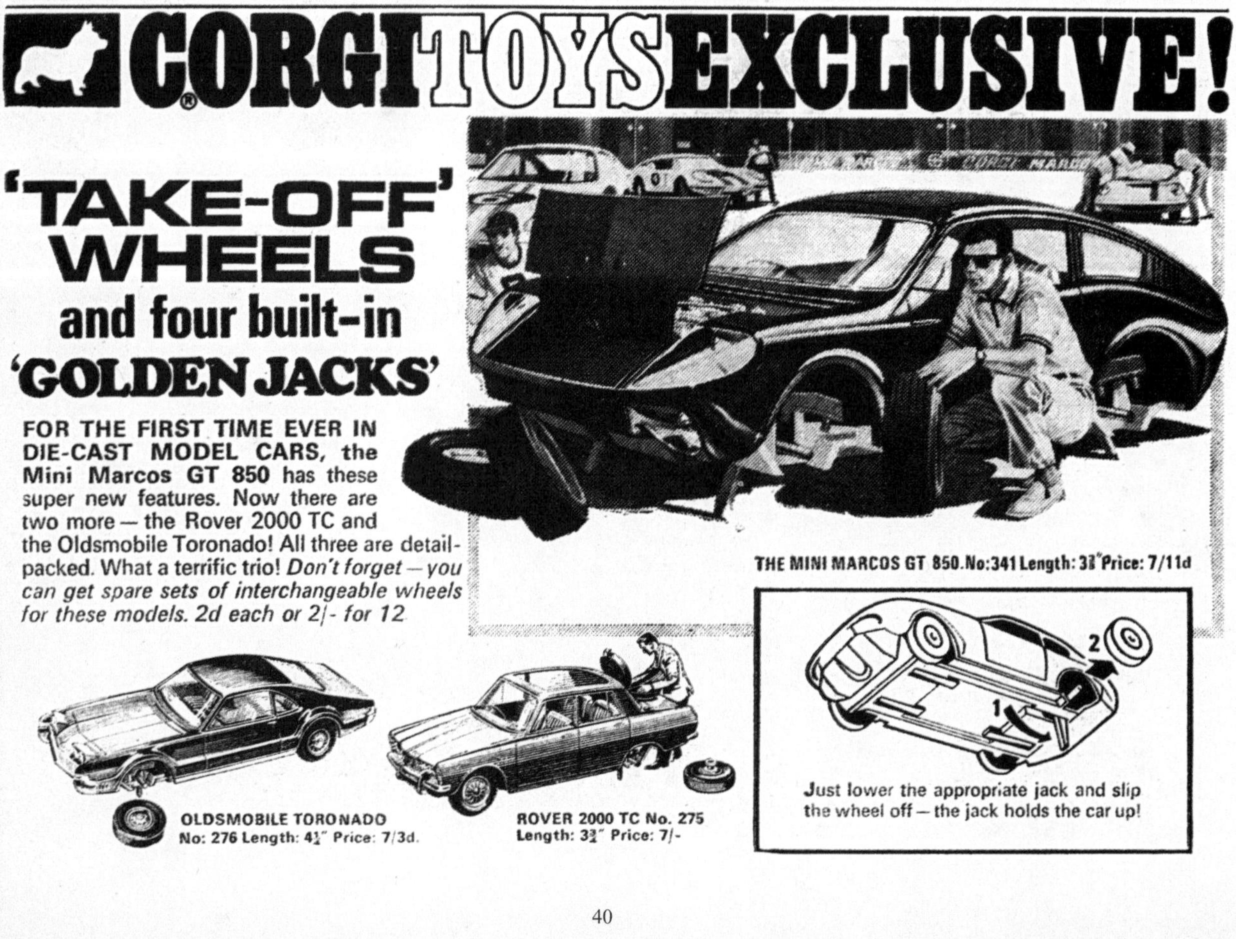
CORGI TOYS EXCLUSIVE!
'TAKE-OFF' WHEELS and four built-in 'GOLDEN JACKS'
FOR THE FIRST TIME EVER IN DIE-CAST MODEL CARS, the Mini Marcos GT 850 has these super new features. Now there are two more — the Rover 2000 TC and the Oldsmobile Toronado! All three are detail-packed. What a terrific trio! Don't forget — you can get spare sets of interchangeable wheels for these models. 2d each or 2/- for 12
THE MINI MARCOS GT 850. No:341 Length: 3⅜" Price: 7/11d
OLDSMOBILE TORONADO No: 276 Length: 4½" Price: 7/3d.
ROVER 2000 TC No. 275 Length: 3¾" Price: 7/-
Just lower the appropriate jack and slip the wheel off — the jack holds the car up!

Roy of the ROVERS

and
THE WINGER FROM THE CIRCUS

By Stewart Colwyn

Roy Race and his pal, Blackie Gray, had been playing in a special practice match to try out a new young right-winger, as Melchester Rovers' first and second team outside-rights were both injured. But the young trialist had proved very disappointing.

THE PALS STARED WIDE-EYED AS THE WIRY LAD DRIBBLED AND SWERVED AROUND HIS BEWILDERED OPPONENTS!

GO IT, CURLY!

HE'S BRILLIANT— BUT THAT BIG CHAP'LL BEAT HIM!

— BUT IT WAS THE BIG CHAP WHO WAS BEATEN!

JUMPING JACKANAPES! HE'S FLICKED IT RIGHT OVER LOFTY'S HEAD! WHAT A WIZARD!

THE YOUNGSTER'S NEXT MOVE WAS ALMOST AS STARTLING. HE ZIPPED ROUND THE BIG LAD, AND CAUGHT THE BALL DEFTLY ON HIS HEAD

WITH THE BALL BOBBING ON HIS HEAD, HE RACED GOALWARDS!

BEFORE ANYONE COULD CHALLENGE HIM, HE NODDED THE BALL NEATLY DOWN TO HIS FEET — AND THEN CRACKED IT THROUGH "THE GOAL"!

GOAL! WHAT A SMASHER!

EXCITEDLY ROY TURNED TO BLACKIE ———

THAT WAS NO FLUKE, BLACKIE! THAT BOY'S A BORN FOOTBALLER! WE'VE GOT TO SPEAK TO HIM — C'MON!

HEY— YOU THERE!

BUT TO THE PALS' ASTONISHMENT, THE LAD DARTED AWAY LIKE A STARTLED HARE

WHAT THE--? COME BACK! WE WANT TO TALK TO YOU!

AN INSTANT LATER THE YOUNG FOOTBALLER WENT CYCLING OFF ALONG A NARROW WALL

THE CRAZY LOON! IF HE COMES OFF, HE'LL BREAK HIS NECK!

BEFORE ROY COULD CALL TO HIM AGAIN, THE LAD HAD VANISHED

HE SEEMED DEAD SCARED OF US, ROY— BUT WHY?

SEARCH ME, BLACKIE! BUT I'M DETERMINED TO FIND HIM AGAIN — LET'S ASK THESE OTHER LADS WHO HE IS!

VOTE FOR PLINGE

TELL US, BOYS —WHO'S THAT LAD IN THE JEANS? WHERE'S HE COME FROM?

FIRST TIME I'VE SEEN HIM— AND THE LAST, BY THE LOOKS OF IT!

HE WHIZZED UP, SAID HE'D ONLY BEEN IN MELCHESTER A FEW HOURS, AND ASKED US IF HE COULD JOIN IN

UNABLE TO LEARN MORE ABOUT THE AMAZING YOUNG FOOTBALLER, ROY AND BLACKIE WALKED AWAY

IT'S INCREDIBLE! WHY SHOULD THAT YOUNG SOCCER GENIUS SUDDENLY VANISH INTO THIN AIR?

BEATS ME, TOO, ROY! THAT LAD'S A BORN BALL JUGGLER — SORT OF CHAP YOU EXPECT TO SEE IN A CIRCUS

A FEW MOMENTS LATER—

BLACKIE — YOU MENTIONED A CIRCUS JUST NOW! BY HARRY I THINK YOU'VE GOT SOMETHING! LOOK!

A MERRY CIRCUS PARADE WAS MOVING DOWN MELCHESTER HIGH STREET!

STRINGER'S CIRCUS
TONIGHT!

SEE WHAT I MEAN, BLACKIE?

BY GOSH, YES — I GET IT! YOU THINK THAT LAD MIGHT BE A CIRCUS JUGGLER?

WHY NOT? LOOK AT THAT CLOWN ON THE POSTER. HE'S JUGGLING — WITH HIS FEET. I RECKON WE'RE ON THE RIGHT TRACK!

STRINGER'S CIRCUS
TONIGHT!

BUT IF THE LAD WORKS IN THE CIRCUS, WHY DID HE BOLT WHEN HE SAW US?

WE DON'T EVEN KNOW HE DOES WORK IN THE CIRCUS — BUT WE CAN SOON FIND OUT!

SO, THAT EVENING, ROY AND BLACKIE VISITED THE CIRCUS—

KEEP YOUR FINGERS CROSSED, BLACKIE—AND WATCH THE JUGGLERS!

SUDDENLY A SPOTLIGHT SWUNG STRAIGHT ON TO THE PALS!

HEY! WHAT'S GOING ON?

NEXT MOMENT, THE VOICE OF THE RINGMASTER RANG OUT—

LADIES AND GENTLEMEN! WE HAVE WITH US TONIGHT THOSE TWO STAR FOOTBALLERS—MELCHESTER'S VERY OWN BLACKIE GRAY AND ROY RACE! GIVE THEM A BIG HAND, FOLKS!

AS THE PALS ACKNOWLEDGED THE APPLAUSE, THEY DID NOT SEE ONE OF THE WAITING PERFORMERS, WHO GAVE A GASP OF RECOGNITION

GOSH, IT'S THOSE TWO CHAPS WHO CALLED OUT TO ME DURING OUR KICK-ABOUT THIS MORNING BEFORE I DASHED OFF! WHAT DO THEY WANT? HAVE THEY FOLLOWED ME HERE?

JUST THEN THE STERN VOICE OF THE RINGMASTER CUT ACROSS THE LAD'S TROUBLED THOUGHTS

DON'T STAND THERE DREAMING, TIM! QUICK— YOU'RE ON!

Y-YES—O.K., MR. STRINGER!

AS THE YOUNG JUGGLER CAME SKIPPING INTO THE RING, ROY NUDGED BLACKIE

LOOK—IT'S HIM— THE LAD FROM THE BOMBSITE! I'D KNOW THAT FANCY HEAD-WORK ANYWHERE!

THE PALS WERE ASTOUNDED AS THE LAD PROCEEDED TO DISPLAY HIS ALMOST UNCANNY SKILL!

THE DELIGHTED ONLOOKERS YELLED THEIR APPLAUSE —

THE BOY'S INCREDIBLE!

I'LL SAY HE IS! I'VE NEVER SEEN ANYTHING LIKE IT!

FROM HIS FOOT, TIM FLICKED THE BALL UPWARDS, CAUGHT IT ON HIS KNEE, AND THEN —

—ALMOST IN THE SAME MOVEMENT, HE FLIPPED IT INTO THE AIR, SWUNG ROUND, AND TRAPPED IT WITH HIS OTHER FOOT!

ROY AND BLACKIE COULD HARDLY BELIEVE THEIR EYES

NO DOUBT ABOUT IT, ROY — THE BOY'S A GENIUS!

WHAT A FOOTBALLER HE'D MAKE!

THE LAD MUST HAVE HEARD ROY'S REMARK, FOR HE SUDDENLY STUMBLED NERVOUSLY — — —

GOSH! I RECKON HE'S RECOGNISED US! IT'S PUT HIM OFF HIS STROKE!

THEN, AS THE BALL SWUNG OVER THE RINGSIDE, ROY JUMPED UP AND DEFTLY NODDED IT STRAIGHT BACK TO JUGGLER TIM!

HOORAY! NICE WORK, ROY!

TRUST THE ROVERS TO SAVE A STICKY SITUATION!

THE ACT ENDED TO ROARS OF APPLAUSE

NOW'S OUR CHANCE TO GET A WORD WITH THAT LAD! C'MON, BLACKIE!

THE YOUNG JUGGLER SAW THE PALS COMING, AND TRIED TO SLIP AWAY, BUT———

HEY—JUST A MINUTE, TIM! WE WANT TO TALK TO YOU!

I CAN'T STOP NOW— PLEASE, LEAVE ME ALONE! IF MR. STRINGER FINDS OUT I'VE BEEN PLAYING FOOTBALL AGAIN, THERE'LL BE TROUBLE!

BUT THE CIRCUS OWNER WAS CLOSE BY AND———

WHAT'S THIS ABOUT FOOTBALL? IS THAT WHY YOU WERE MISSING FROM THE PARADE THIS MORNING? I WARNED YOU WHAT WOULD HAPPEN IF———

Y—YES, MR. STRINGER, I'M SORRY!

MYSTIFIED BY THE RINGMASTER'S HOSTILE MANNER, ROY CUT IN———

I DON'T UNDERSTAND ALL THIS, MR. STRINGER, BUT PERHAPS YOU DON'T REALISE THAT TIM'S A BORN FOOTBALLER. BLACKIE AND I CAME ALONG THIS EVENING TO INVITE HIM TO SIGN ON FOR MELCHESTER ROVERS

NOT IF I KNOW IT, MR. RACE. TIM'S CAREER IS IN THE CIRCUS, LIKE HIS FATHER BEFORE HIM, AND THIS IS WHERE HE STAYS. HE'S MY STAR ACT!

DESPERATELY ROY LOOKED AROUND. SUDDENLY HE SPOTTED THE BIG TOP'S EMPTY SEATS!

BUT EVEN TIM'S WONDERFUL ACT ISN'T PACKING THE HOUSE, IS IT? LISTEN CHIEF! IF WE CAN WORK UP A TURN TO BRING IN THE CUSTOMERS IN A BIG WAY, WILL YOU LET TIM PLAY IN A TRIAL GAME WITH THE ROVERS?

"BUSINESS IS CERTAINLY NOT GOOD. PEOPLE DON'T SEEM TO WANT THE CIRCUS THESE DAYS. O.K., MR. RACE. IF YOU CAN BRING ME SOME FULL HOUSES, I'LL AGREE TO YOUR PROPOSAL!"

TIM'S EYES SPARKLED—

"DON'T WORRY, TIM. MAYBE YOU'LL BE GETTING YOUR CHANCE TO PLAY FOOTBALL QUICKER THAN YOU THINK!"

"GEE, MR. RACE—THANKS!"

THE PALS HURRIED BACK TO THE STADIUM, AND FOUND MANY OF THE ROVERS IN THE CLUB ROOM

"HEY, THERE, YOU BLOKES! BLACKIE AND I NEED YOUR HELP"

"O.K., ROY! WHAT'S IN THE AIR?"

BRIEFLY, ROVERS CENTRE-FORWARD OUTLINED HIS SCHEME

"THAT STUNT OF YOURS OUGHT TO DRAW THE CROWDS, ROY!"

"WE'RE ALL WITH YOU! IT'LL BE GRAND FUN!"

THE FOLLOWING EVENING, CROWDS FLOCKED TO STRINGER'S CIRCUS——

"THEY SAY THIS NEW MYSTERY ACT IS GOING TO BE HOT-STUFF!"

"I CAN'T WAIT TO SEE WHAT IT'S ALL ABOUT!"

STRINGER'S CIRCUS NEW! TONIGHT! SENSATIONAL MYSTERY ACT!

THE CROWDS HADN'T LONG TO WAIT ——

LADIES AND GENTLEMEN! INTRODUCING A GRAND NEW, BRAND-NEW CIRCUS GAME, WHICH I KNOW YOU'LL ENJOY. IT FEATURES YOUR GREAT FAVOURITES —— THE MELCHESTER ROVERS! HERE THEY COME ——!

IN RACED THE ROVERS —— ON STILTS!

ROY AND HIS PALS WERE SOON PLAYING THEIR AMAZING STILT-SOCCER MATCH!

HOORAY! IT'S A GOAL! ONE TO US!

COME ON, ROY! UP THE ROVERS!

NO GOAL! I WAS SWEPT OFF MY FEET!

THE AUDIENCE WENT WILD WITH DELIGHT AT THE ROVERS' ANTICS

HA HA! WHAT A SUPER SHOW!

ROVERS OUGHT TO PACK THE PLACE OUT EVERY NIGHT WITH THAT ACT!

MR. STRINGER WAS MORE THAN DELIGHTED

THE ACT'S A WINNER ALL THE WAY! ROY AND THE OTHER ROVERS HAVE SAVED THE DAY FOR ME! THEY'RE A GRAND BUNCH OF LADS!

49

AND SO, AS ROY LED HIS TEAM OUT OF THE RING —

WONDERFUL, ROY! YOU KEPT YOUR WORD, AND I'LL KEEP MINE. TIM CAN PLAY IN YOUR SOCCER TRIAL — AND I WISH HIM LUCK!

THAT'S GREAT NEWS, MR. STRINGER! WELL, TIM, YOU'VE GOT YOUR CHANCE — NOW IT'S UP TO YOU!

NEXT DAY, TIM TURNED UP AT ROVERS' STADIUM FOR THE VITAL TRIAL ———

NOW DON'T BE NERVOUS, TIM. I KNOW YOU CAN MAKE IT, BLACKIE AND I WILL HELP YOU ALL WE CAN. GOOD LUCK, LAD

THANKS, MR. RACE. I'LL DO MY BEST!

AT LAST, THE GAME STARTED, AND TENSELY BLACKIE WATCHED ROY MOVE AWAY... SOON ROY SWUNG THE BALL OUT TO TIM —

NOW WE'LL SEE WHAT YOUNG TIM REALLY CAN DO!

BUT BEFORE THE CIRCUS-LAD COULD TRAP THE BALL —

HE'S ROBBED! NOT QUITE QUICK ENOUGH — BUT HE'LL BE O.K.

SEVERAL TIMES DURING THE NEXT FEW MINUTES, ROY TRIED TO GIVE TIM A CHANCE TO SHOW HIS WONDERFUL BALL JUGGLERY, BUT EACH TIME HE WAS BEATEN BY THE DEFENDERS

BAD LUCK, LAD!

EVEN WHEN TIM DID MANAGE TO "JUGGLE" HIS WAY PAST THE FULL-BACK, HIS FINAL PASS TO ROY WAS WELL OUT OF RANGE

YOU'LL NEVER GET THAT PASS, ROY!

YOUNG TIM'S NOT DOING TOO WELL, ROY. HE SEEMS UNABLE TO SETTLE DOWN!

SOMETHING'S MAKING HIM JUMPY. I'M SURE IT'S NOT NERVES!

SUDDENLY ROY SPOTTED A FIGURE STANDING WATCHING THE TRIAL

LOOK, BLACKIE! THERE'S MR. STRINGER, THE CIRCUS BOSS. THAT'S WHAT'S GIVING TIM THE JITTERS!

NEXT TIME THERE WAS A BRIEF BREAK, THE PALS MOVED ACROSS TO TIM

RELAX, TIM. DON'T WORRY ABOUT MR. STRINGER. SHOW HIM THE WAY YOU PLAYED THAT MORNING ON THE BOMBSITE. THAT'S ALL YOU HAVE TO DO!

O.K. SORRY, MR. RACE. HECK— I KEEP THINKING HE'S GOING TO BAWL ME OUT FOR PLAYING SOCCER AGAIN!

FROM THEN ON, THE CIRCUS LAD REALLY DID SHOW SOME OF HIS AMAZING TRICKS —

BRILLIANT PASS! THAT'S MUCH MORE LIKE IT!

ROY COULD HAVE SHOT, BUT INSTEAD HE SLIPPED THE BALL BACK TO TIM

MUST GIVE HIM A CHANCE TO SHOW WHAT HE CAN DO!

CONTROLLING THE BALL WITH MASTERFUL PRECISION, TIM BEAT ONE OPPONENT AFTER ANOTHER!

THEN, WITH THE BALL BOUNCING ON HIS HEAD, TIM COMPLETELY BAMBOOZLED THE LEFT BACK!

NEXT MOMENT, HE FLICKED THE BALL BACK TO HIS FOOT, AND HIT IT FIRST TIME!

GOAL! A BEAUTY, TIM!

NO CIRCUS STUNT ABOUT THAT SHOT!

MANAGER BEN GALLOWAY AND THE ROVERS DIRECTORS WERE DELIGHTED

WHAT AN AMAZING DISPLAY, BEN!

YOU'RE TELLING ME! LOOKS AS IF WE'VE FOUND THE RIGHT-WINGER WE WANT— THANKS TO ROY! I'M SIGNING THAT BOY BEFORE SOME OTHER CLUB SPOTS HIM!

AFTER THE GAME, MR. STRINGER HURRIED FORWARD TO CONGRATULATE TIM

ROY WAS RIGHT, TIM — YOU'RE A BORN FOOTBALLER. I'M ONLY SORRY THAT WHEN THE CIRCUS MOVES ON FROM MELCHESTER I SHALL HAVE TO FIND A NEW STAR ACT. BUT BEST OF LUCK IN YOUR SOCCER CAREER WITH THE ROVERS!

THANKS, MR. STRINGER. I'LL NEVER LET YOU—OR THEM— DOWN!

LATER, AS ROY, BLACKIE AND TIM LEFT MELCHESTER STADIUM —

ONE AT A TIME, BOYS! HERE— GET THE AUTOGRAPH OF ROVERS' NEW RIGHT-WINGER!

GO ON, TIM! YOU'LL HAVE TO GET USED TO THIS SORT OF THING!

THE END

SPEND a WEEK with ROY RACE

Don't envy young Peter Simpson being invited to spend a whole week with Roy and the Rovers. You can join him—

SUNDAY

PETER ARRIVED AT ROY'S HOME ON SUNDAY AFTERNOON AND THEY SPENT THE EVENING LOOKING THROUGH PROGRAMMES AND NEWSPAPER CUTTINGS OF ROVERS' MATCHES.

WHAT A FINE COLLECTION OF PROGRAMMES, MR. RACE

YES, ROY'S KEPT ONE OF EACH MATCH IN WHICH HE'S PLAYED

MONDAY

IN THE MORNING, ROY TOOK PETER TO THE ROVERS' GROUND TO MEET BLACKIE AND TO WATCH THE PLAYERS PUTTING IN A SPELL OF LIGHT TRAINING ON THE PRACTICE PITCH.

WE DON'T DO MUCH MORE THAN A FEW LAPS ON MONDAYS. SHAN'T BE LONG ———!

O.K. ROY

COME ON, SLACKER!

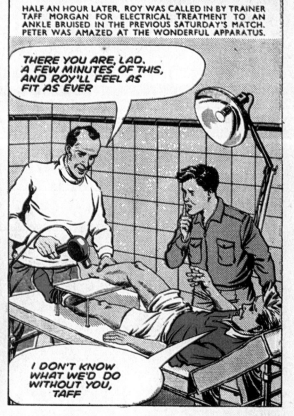

HALF AN HOUR LATER, ROY WAS CALLED IN BY TRAINER TAFF MORGAN FOR ELECTRICAL TREATMENT TO AN ANKLE BRUISED IN THE PREVIOUS SATURDAY'S MATCH. PETER WAS AMAZED AT THE WONDERFUL APPARATUS.

THERE YOU ARE, LAD. A FEW MINUTES OF THIS, AND ROY'LL FEEL AS FIT AS EVER

I DON'T KNOW WHAT WE'D DO WITHOUT YOU, TAFF

AFTER LUNCH, ROY, BLACKIE AND PETER WENT ALONG TO THE LOCAL SWIMMING BATH. SOME OF THE OTHER ROVERS WERE THERE, TOO, AND THE FUN WAS FAST AND FURIOUS—ESPECIALLY WHEN THEY PLAYED A SCRATCH WATER-POLO MATCH.

GO ON, ROY— SHOOT! *GOAL!*

FOUL! OFFSIDE! TURN HIM OUT!

THAT EVENING, BLACKIE INVITED ROY AND PETER TO HIS LODGINGS TO SEE SOME OF THE CINE-FILMS HE HAD TAKEN OF THE ROVERS ON TOUR. PETER WAS THRILLED—

THAT'S ROY AND SOME OF THE LADS SEEING THE SIGHTS IN SPAIN

TUESDAY

IN THE MORNING THE ROVERS GOT DOWN TO SERIOUS TRAINING AND WENT FOR A 10-MILE RUN IN THE COUNTRY. PETER WANTED TO JOIN IN, BUT ROY BORROWED A BIKE FOR HIM.

PHEW! WHO'D BE A FOOTBALLER?

HEY, ROY—WHY DIDN'T YOU HIRE BIKES FOR ALL OF US?

WHEN THEY RETURNED TO THE STADIUM, MANAGER BEN GALLOWAY HAD ARRANGED FOR A LOCAL PRESS PHOTOGRAPHER TO TAKE A TEAM-GROUP. PETER COULDN'T JOIN THAT!

BETTER TAKE ME ON MY OWN, THESE OTHER CHAPS WILL BURST YOUR CAMERA!

THAT AFTERNOON, ROY TOOK PETER WITH HIM ON HIS MOTOR SCOOTER TO HIS OLD SCHOOL WHERE HE GAVE A WEEKLY COACHING SESSION TO THE BOYS.

BY THE TIME THEY RETURNED HOME, ROY WAS TOO TIRED TO GO OUT AGAIN, SO, AS THERE WAS A FOOTBALL MATCH ON THE TELEVISION, THEY STAYED IN TO WATCH IT

NICE WORK — NOW THEN — ON YOUR OWN!

WEDNESDAY IN THE MORNING, ROVERS HELD THEIR WEEKLY PRACTICE MATCH—FIRST TEAM AGAINST RESERVES. IT WAS SERIOUS FOOTBALL, AND PETER WAS THRILLED AS HE WATCHED—AND LISTENED TO THE COACH GIVING ADVICE

RIGHT-BACK—MOVE IN TO TACKLE!

GOSH! I WISH I COULD PLAY LIKE ROY!

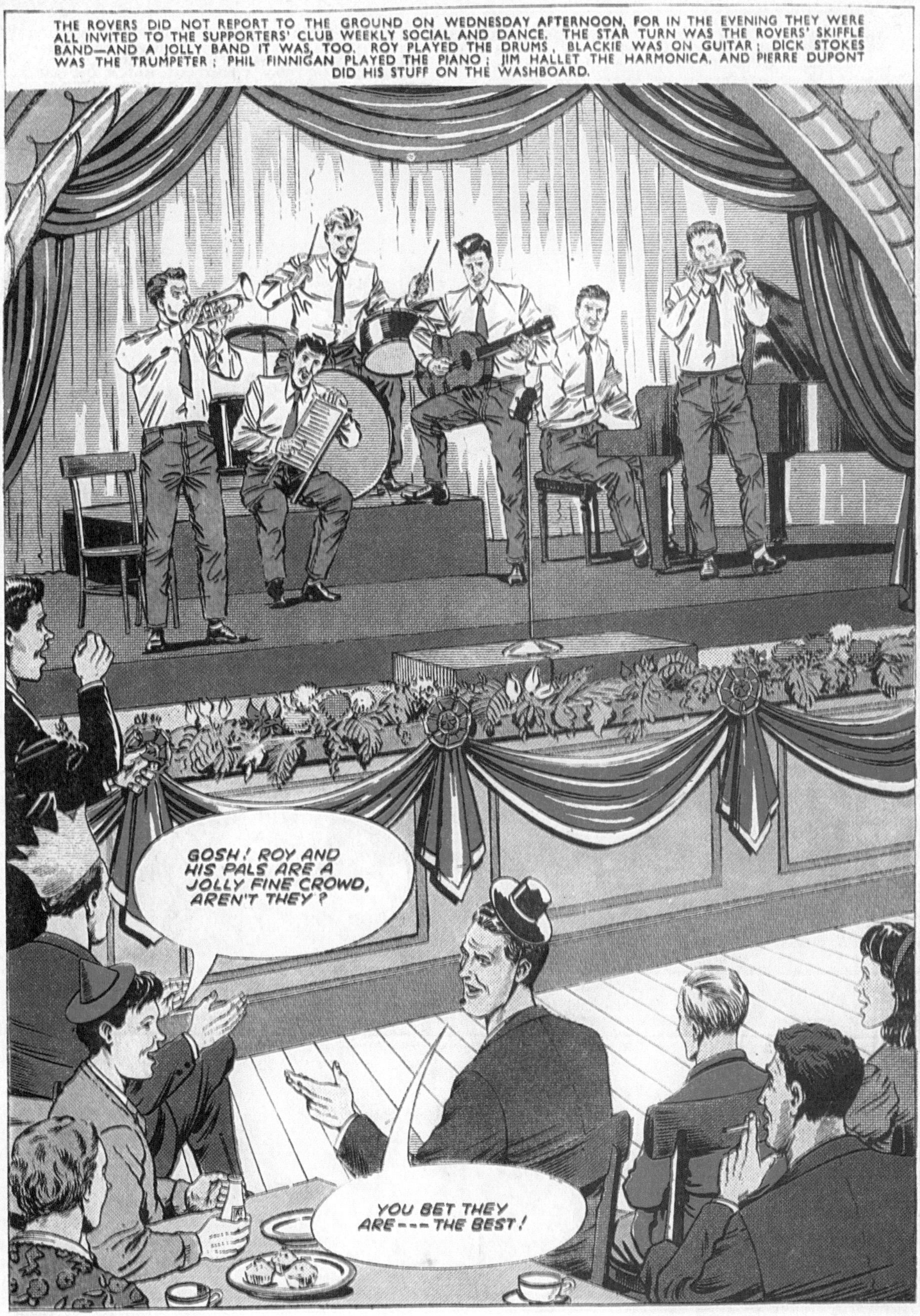
THE ROVERS DID NOT REPORT TO THE GROUND ON WEDNESDAY AFTERNOON, FOR IN THE EVENING THEY WERE ALL INVITED TO THE SUPPORTERS' CLUB WEEKLY SOCIAL AND DANCE. THE STAR TURN WAS THE ROVERS' SKIFFLE BAND—AND A JOLLY BAND IT WAS, TOO. ROY PLAYED THE DRUMS, BLACKIE WAS ON GUITAR; DICK STOKES WAS THE TRUMPETER; PHIL FINNIGAN PLAYED THE PIANO; JIM HALLET THE HARMONICA, AND PIERRE DUPONT DID HIS STUFF ON THE WASHBOARD.
GOSH! ROY AND HIS PALS ARE A JOLLY FINE CROWD, AREN'T THEY?
YOU BET THEY ARE --- THE BEST!

THURSDAY

THE ROVERS WERE OUT BRIGHT AND EARLY THE NEXT MORNING. FOR THE FIRST HOUR THEY ENTERED INTO SOME STRENUOUS TEAM GAMES—AND THE COACH ALLOWED PETER TO JOIN IN.

COME ON, PETER—QUICK! WE'RE WINNING!

GET A MOVE ON! FASTER!

AFTER A BRIEF BREAK, THE PLAYERS HURRIED OFF TO THE PRACTICE GROUND FOR SOME BALL-WORK. THE PART THAT PETER ENJOYED MOST WAS THE RAPID-FIRE SHOOTING PRACTICE BY ROY AND THE OTHER FORWARDS. ABOUT A DOZEN BALLS WERE USED, AND THE ROVERS HAD TO HIT THEM FIRST TIME, FROM ALL ANGLES. IT WAS TERRIFIC!

GO ON, PETER! HAVE A SHOT YOURSELF! HIT IT!

IN THE EVENING, MOST OF THE ROVERS WENT ALONG TO A LOCAL FACTORY FOR A SERIES OF MATCHES AGAINST THE WORKS SPORTS TEAM. ROY CAPTAINED THE ROVERS AT BADMINTON AND TABLE TENNIS, WHILE BLACKIE LED THE DARTS TEAM, AND HUGHIE GRIFFITHS THE SNOOKER TEAM. IT WAS ALL JOLLY GOOD FUN, AND THE ROVERS LADS JUST MANAGED TO WIN THE EVENING'S SPORT—THANKS TO ROY'S TABLE TENNIS VICTORY OVER THE LOCAL CHAMPION.

DOUBLE TOP! BLACKIE'S IN FORM TO-NIGHT

FRIDAY

NO STRENUOUS TRAINING TODAY, EXCEPT P.T., FOLLOWED BY WEIGHT-LIFTING EXERCISES. PETER WAS AMAZED AT THIS, BUT ROY TOLD HIM THAT IT IS NOW A REGULAR FEATURE OF ROVERS' TRAINING.

PHEW! THIS IS GRAND TRAINING—PETER!

KEEP IT UP, ROY!

THE MORNING'S WORK FINISHED WITH THE WEEKLY MEDICAL EXAMINATION BY THE CLUB'S DOCTOR. BUT, AS USUAL, THE DOC. HAD TO ADMIT THAT THE ROVERS' FIRST-TEAMERS WERE AS FIT AS FIDDLES!

O.K., ROY! NOTHING WRONG WITH YOU!

FRIDAY AFTERNOON WAS GIVEN OVER TO A TACTICAL TALK ABOUT THE FOLLOWING DAY'S MATCH. PETER WAS ALLOWED TO GO ALONG, AND SAT LISTENING INTENTLY AS ASSISTANT-MANAGER ANDY McDONALD, THE COACH, AND THE TRAINER, DISCUSSED TACTICS WITH THE PLAYERS.

ROY, PETER AND BLACKIE WENT STRAIGHT HOME—FOR A QUIET EVENING. IT IS A CLUB RULE THAT THE PLAYERS TAKE THINGS EASY ON FRIDAY EVENINGS, AND GET TO BED EARLY

TIME I WAS GOING. WE'VE GOT A HARD MATCH TO-MORROW. SEE YOU IN THE MORNING, PETER!

SATURDAY

HOW PROUD PETER FELT AS HE STROLLED DOWN TO THE STADIUM WITH ROY AND BLACKIE.

BEST OF LUCK THIS AFTERNOON, ROY AND BLACKIE! WE'LL BE THERE!

AFTER LUNCHING WITH THE ROVERS, PETER WAS TAKEN ALONG TO THE DRESSING-ROOM, WHERE EVERYTHING WAS READY FOR THE PLAYERS.

GOSH, ROY, DOESN'T THE PLACE LOOK SMART?

YES—TAFF AND HIS STAFF HAVE BEEN BUSY ALL THE MORNING.

PETER HAD TO LEAVE WHEN THE OTHER LADS ARRIVED. NO ONE BUT PLAYERS AND OFFICIALS ARE ALLOWED IN THE DRESSING-ROOMS ON MATCH-DAY

ANDY'LL LOOK AFTER YOU, PETER. SEE YOU AFTER THE GAME

GOOD LUCK, ROY! MIND YOU WIN!

WHEN THE GAME STARTED, PETER HAD A SEAT ON THE TRAINERS' BENCH, ALONG WITH ANDY McDONALD, ROVERS' ASSISTANT-MANAGER, AND WHEN ROY OPENED THE SCORING WITH A BRILLIANT GOAL, PETER YELLED HIS HEAD OFF!

GOAL! GOOD OLD ROY! UP THE ROVERS!

ROY SCORED TWICE MORE, AND THE ROVERS CAME OFF AT THE END 3—0 WINNERS. PETER RACED FORWARD TO GREET HIS PAL..

JOLLY GOOD GAME, ROY! WELL DONE!

I RECKON WE'D BETTER ADOPT YOU AS OUR LUCKY MASCOT, PETER!

THE MATCH OVER, PETER WAS ALLOWED TO GO INTO THE DRESSING-ROOM FOR HE WAS NOW A GREAT FAVOURITE WITH ALL THE ROVERS. AS A MEMENTO, THEY ALL AUTOGRAPHED THE BALL THEY HAD USED IN THEIR VICTORY, AND PRESENTED IT TO HIM.

WE HOPE YOU WILL KEEP THIS BALL, PETER, TO REMIND YOU OF YOUR WEEK WITH THE ROVERS. IT'S BEEN GRAND HAVING YOU WITH US!

GOSH, THANKS!

THAT EVENING, THE VICTORIOUS ROVERS WERE ENTERTAINED TO TEA AT THE SUPPORTERS CLUB, WHERE PETER WAS MADE CHIEF GUEST. BUT THE TIME CAME FOR HIM TO LEAVE FOR HIS HOME, SO PETER HAD TO SAY "CHEERIO" TO ALL THE MANY NEW PALS HE HAD MADE DURING A WEEK HE WOULD NEVER FORGET!

A DAY WITH THE F.A.

Everybody knows that F.A. stands for the Football Association that organises and controls all Soccer played in England. But have you any idea how this colossal task is carried out?

I thought I'd find out for myself—and take all of YOU with me. So join me on a "Skipper conducted tour" of the home of the F.A. at 22 Russell Square in the heart of London's West End.

There's no mistaking the F.A. building. As you can see by the above photo, the England badge is prominent above the imposing entrance. But once you step inside the palatial entrance hall, you feel the atmosphere of football all round you.

Everywhere you go within the building there are photographs of football—team groups, portraits of famous players, and trophies by the hundred. On the ground floor is the busy main office, where much of the daily routine work is done. It was here that I met Mr. Bird, whose chief job is arranging the referees and linesmen for ALL League and Cup games, amateur and professional, throughout the whole season. You can imagine what a whole-time job this is for dedicated Mr. Bird.

Next door is the Committee Room. All the chairs in there were presented by the Scottish, Irish, and Welsh F.A.s and each chair is carved with one of the badges.

Nearby, on the ground floor, is the F.A. Council Chamber, where all the big meetings are held. But we'll visit that later. Meanwhile, let's go upstairs—past more glass cases of trophies, to another block of offices. In one room I met Mr. Odell whose job it is to make all the arrangements for English international teams and F.A. representative sides—travel, hotels, tickets, etc.—both at home and overseas.

Then I called into the offices of the England manager, Sir Alf Ramsey; Mr. Hughes, who looks after amateur internationals, and Mr. Wade, the chief of the coaching side of the F.A. They are three very important members of the staff, for each plays a big part in developing young players.

My next call was to the office of the man who is in charge—Mr. Denis Follows, the F.A. Secretary. "Glad to see you," he greeted me with the beaming smile that

has made him so well liked. " Sit down and have some tea."

Then, despite the pile of papers on his desk and dozens of letters to be read and answered, just a small part of his duties, Mr. Follows sat talking football for at least half an hour. What an interesting man he is. A former schoolmaster, he knew all about Roy of the Rovers and Tiger and Hurricane—but then he's a real football enthusiast.

In the photograph of him (above) you can see at least some of the many trophies that surround his large office. On the mantelpiece is a replica of the World Cup; ashtrays from the Brazil F.A.; a Footballer of the Year trophy, and a framed badge of the 1966 World Cup.

Many of the framed photographs around the walls of his office were taken by Mr. Follows himself and enlarged—pictures of famous foreign Soccer grounds. But another of the frames contains a beautiful certificate awarded to the F.A. of England by FIFA to commemorate winning the World Cup at Wembley. It's surrounded by the coloured flags of the 16 countries who played in the 1966 Finals.

Before I left Mr. Follows I asked him for a brief personal message which I could pass on to you all.

" Only too pleased," he replied with a smile.

So here it is, from the F.A. Secretary himself.

SPECIAL MESSAGE TO ALL OUR READERS FROM THE SECRETARY OF THE F.A.

"1966 was a very proud year for English football. To win the World Championship and the Jules Rimet Cup was probably the greatest sporting achievement of this country in the present century. But remember, the Cup was won as a result of the efforts of eleven English footballers, assisted by their manager and trainers, a wonderful effort indeed. Some years ago each member of the successful England team was a schoolboy, just as you are today. That fact should be an inspiring example to you and encourage you to improve your skills and knowledge of the game so that perhaps in ten or twelve years' time YOU may be a member of another successful England World Cup side.

"The best of good luck to you all.
"DENIS FOLLOWS
"Secretary Football Association."

Above is the spacious F.A. Council Chamber where all the very important meetings are held. In the centre is the chair on which sits the Chairman of the Association, while around the walls are photographs of all the men who have held this high office since the F.A. began in 1863.

It is here in the Council Chamber that all the draws are made for F.A. Cup and Amateur Cup-ties. On these occasions this historic room is packed with Pressmen and club managers.

The draw is made by picking numbered balls from a mauve velvet bag, the numbers corresponding with the names of the clubs involved which are written down on a numbered list before the draw.

I had the great thrill of handling the velvet bag and one of the boxes of numbered balls (picture on left).

ENGLAND

SOCCER STORES

In the basement of the F.A. headquarters I found perhaps the most fascinating of all the departments that make up this amazing organisation. It's the department that handles all the kit and medical requirements for England's international teams: Youth, amateur, Under-23 and senior sides.

Mr. Bill Deaton and Mr. Bayliss showed me around. They were busy packing the kit for one of the England team's home games—and I could hardly believe my own eyes!

Each player in the party—usually 22 of them, including the reserves—must have FIVE complete sets of kit. Three are for training and the other two for the actual game. A set includes five shirts, shorts, pairs of socks, and underpants, and two track suits, one for training and the other to wear when the team takes the field for the big match. The two trainers and the manager also need track suits. Goalies' sweaters, too, of course.

All this kit has to be carefully packed into big hamper baskets. But that isn't all. At least twelve footballs must be included and, of course, all the other small items that are so essential to footballers—rolls of cotton wool, bandages, jars of grease and even hair oil! Another basket is packed with several dozen towels.

The rooms in the basement of the F.A. headquarters look like a big department store, with all the various items stacked neatly away on shelves. In the corner of one room is a huge cupboard for all the medical supplies —talk about a chemist's shop!

Another thing that interested me was the leather trainer's bag. (That's a close-up picture of it on the right.) It contains 48 different articles, all vitally necessary for the comfort of the players and the treatment of their knocks and minor injuries. By the way, the spotted bag you can see in the bottom of the picture contains the " magic sponge ".

As I wandered around among all the piles of kit I spotted a box containing brand new blue and gold international caps. No, they weren't being packed with the other kit. Mr. Bayliss explained that the caps are sent to each player after matches by registered post.

SKIPPER tests a training football before it is packed with other international kit. (Below) The trainer's bag all ready for use.

This is just a small section of the files containing the full records of every footballer in England. SKIPPER tells you below about his visit to this important department of the F.A.

THEY'RE ALL HERE

Did you know that the Football Association have a complete record of every player appearing in top class amateur and professional Soccer in England? It's true. I saw it for myself during my visit to F.A. headquarters.

The Registry Department is run by Mr. Hawes and Mr. Gilbert, and you can take it from me it's a most important job. Around the walls of their offices are rows of filing cabinets containing the particulars of every player—when he signed on, his transfers, cautions by referees—everything in fact about his career.

The files contain the records of about 11,500 footballers, from 1946 to the present time, so you can guess the terrific amount of work that is needed to keep the files up to date.

While I was there Mr. Hawes was handed a telegram from a well-known League club stating that they had just secured the transfer of a player. The transfer forms were in the post. So into the file of that player went the record of his transfer. Just one small item in a very busy day's work for the staff of the F.A. Registry Dept., a job that is never ending.

Mr. Carr (left) is the man who looks after all the publicity work of the F.A. He is also Editor of the monthly F.A. News. In his office he has a copy of almost every book published about football. Another of Mr. Carr's jobs is to answer all the queries sent to the F.A.— dozens every day!

TROPHIES GALORE

I told you earlier on that there are hundreds of interesting trophies to be seen at F.A. headquarters. Many of them are stacked away in cupboards and glass cases because there isn't the room to display all of them properly.

There are cases full of wonderful, beautifully-coloured pennants like those in this picture (right). All have been presented to England captains before international games played all over the world.

I saw dozens of cups, too. One of these (picture right) caught my eye. It was the ORIGINAL F.A. CUP, the one that was stolen in 1895 and never recovered! Then I saw the inscription on it—it was a replica of the first F.A. Cup, presented to the F.A. by Manchester United.

D'you see that queer-looking trophy in the bottom right-hand corner? It's a real, hand-carved totem and was presented to the F.A. team that toured British Columbia in 1950.

The picture at the foot of this column doesn't appear to have much to do with Soccer, does it? But it's one of the first things you see when you step into the F.A. Council Chamber. The head of that ferocious-looking tiger stands on an elephant foot and in front is a beautiful leopard's skin. Mr. Carr told me that these were all presented to the F.A. party that toured South Africa and Rhodesia in 1957.

Wonderful trophies from all over the world of football.

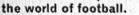

The Mersey Soccer Sound

"EV-ER-TON"
"LIV-ER-POOL"

THE people of Merseyside have two great interests—the Beatles "Tops of the Pops," and Everton and Liverpool "Tops of Soccer."

Those two great clubs have been in the forefront of British football for many years but Liverpool started the modern Mersey craze for Soccer when they won the Second Division Championship in 1962. Twelve months later their near neighbours and rivals Everton carried off the League Championship. Then, determined to add to the glory of Merseyside, Liverpool took the title from Everton in 1964, to complete an incredible hat-trick of honours for the city.

No wonder the Soccer-crazy fans of Liverpool and Everton are proud of their favourites, whose wonderful grounds are within shouting distance of each other.

Everton started in 1878 as "St. Domingo FC" They played at Anfield. But in 1892 Everton (as they had become) refused to pay extra rent and half the club walked out and restarted at Goodison Park. Those who remained at Anfield decided to form a new club and called themselves Liverpool. So that's how Merseyside got TWO clubs instead of one.

Here's a picture you don't often see—two teams for the price of one! (Above) Everton on the left and Liverpool, pose for the cameras before the start of a local Derby at Goodison Park in 1964. When the Reds meet the Blues the Mersey sound can be heard for miles around Lancashire!

Five of Everton's 1963 League Champions with the trophy. Left to right : (back) Derek Temple and Roy Vernon, skipper of that great team ; (front) Denis Stevens, Alex Scott and Alex Young.

SWING-TIME for Ray Wilson, Everton's English international full-back. He's a great favourite with the Goodison fans.

HOORAY FOR THE REDS—led by their mighty Scots skipper Ron Yeats. The genial six-footer is a tower of strength to Liverpool.

"I've got a plan . . ." Ian St. John (centre) discusses match-winning tactics with his Liverpool chums John Chisnall (left) and Gordon Wallace.

THE STORY OF SPURS

The Fabulous Club that Started with an Idea, Hope, and a Hero to Worship–Harry Hotspur!

An everyday sight in the Tottenham High Road in 1882—schoolmates gathered under a street lamp! Yet this group here was forming a now-famous club !

They needed a name for their club, and one boy remembered the story of Henry Percy (Harry Hotspur), who fought and died at the Battle of Shrewsbury. "Why not call ourselves Hotspur?" he suggested—and everyone agreed.

Their next move was to buy a football. Every member of the club paid a shilling.

COME ON. DIG DEEP. A BOB EACH

They took an open pitch on Tottenham marshes, and it was there that the new Hotspur F.C. played their first matches. No one realised in those days that the club was destined for greatness!

The father of a player made their goalposts. After each game the lads carted them to the nearby railway station.

WE'LL COLLECT THEM AGAIN NEXT SATURDAY, SIR

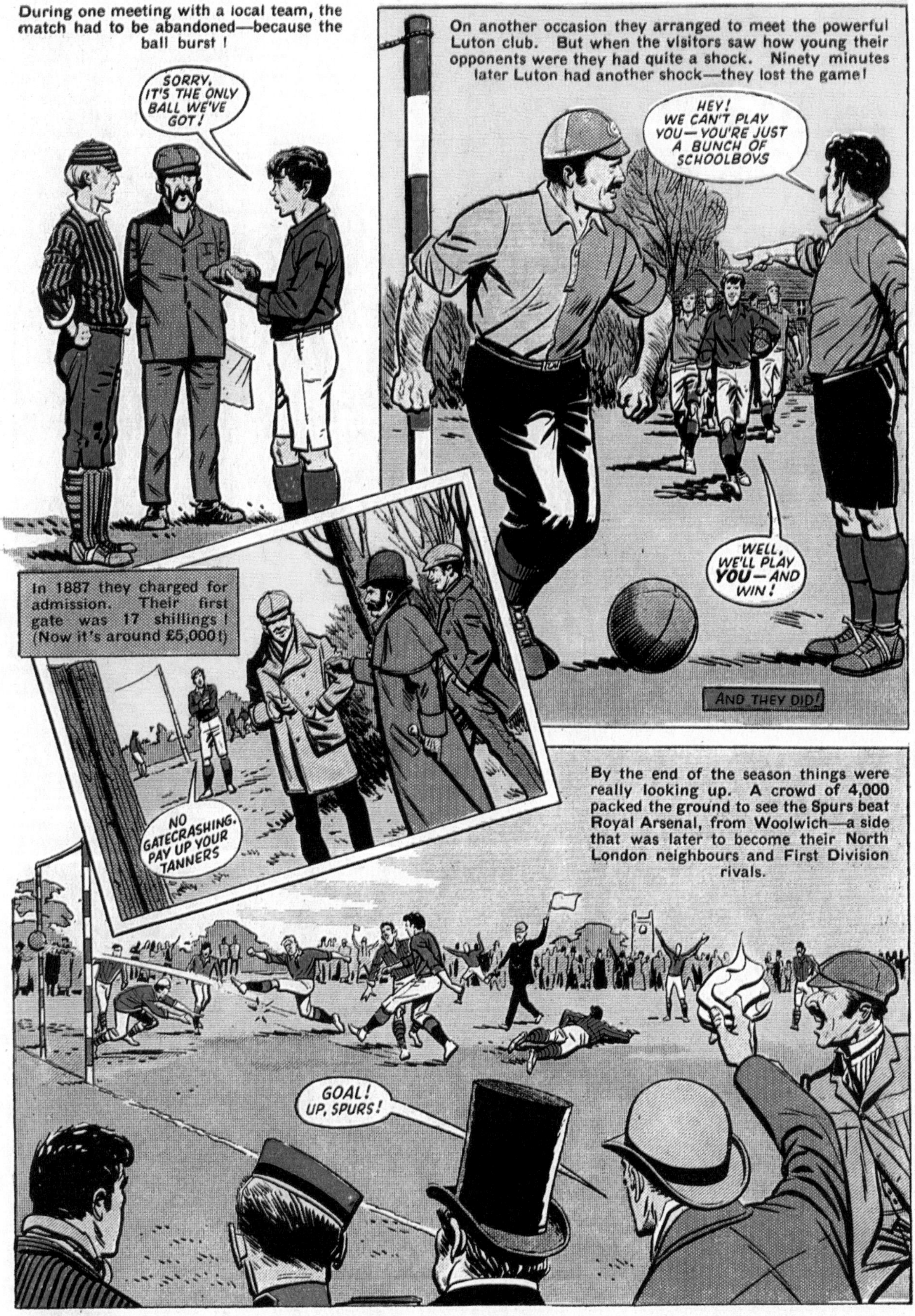
During one meeting with a local team, the match had to be abandoned—because the ball burst !
SORRY. IT'S THE ONLY BALL WE'VE GOT!
On another occasion they arranged to meet the powerful Luton club. But when the visitors saw how young their opponents were they had quite a shock. Ninety minutes later Luton had another shock—they lost the game!
HEY! WE CAN'T PLAY YOU—YOU'RE JUST A BUNCH OF SCHOOLBOYS
WELL, WE'LL PLAY YOU—AND WIN!
AND THEY DID!
In 1887 they charged for admission. Their first gate was 17 shillings ! (Now it's around £5,000!)
NO GATECRASHING. PAY UP YOUR TANNERS
By the end of the season things were really looking up. A crowd of 4,000 packed the ground to see the Spurs beat Royal Arsenal, from Woolwich—a side that was later to become their North London neighbours and First Division rivals.
GOAL! UP, SPURS!

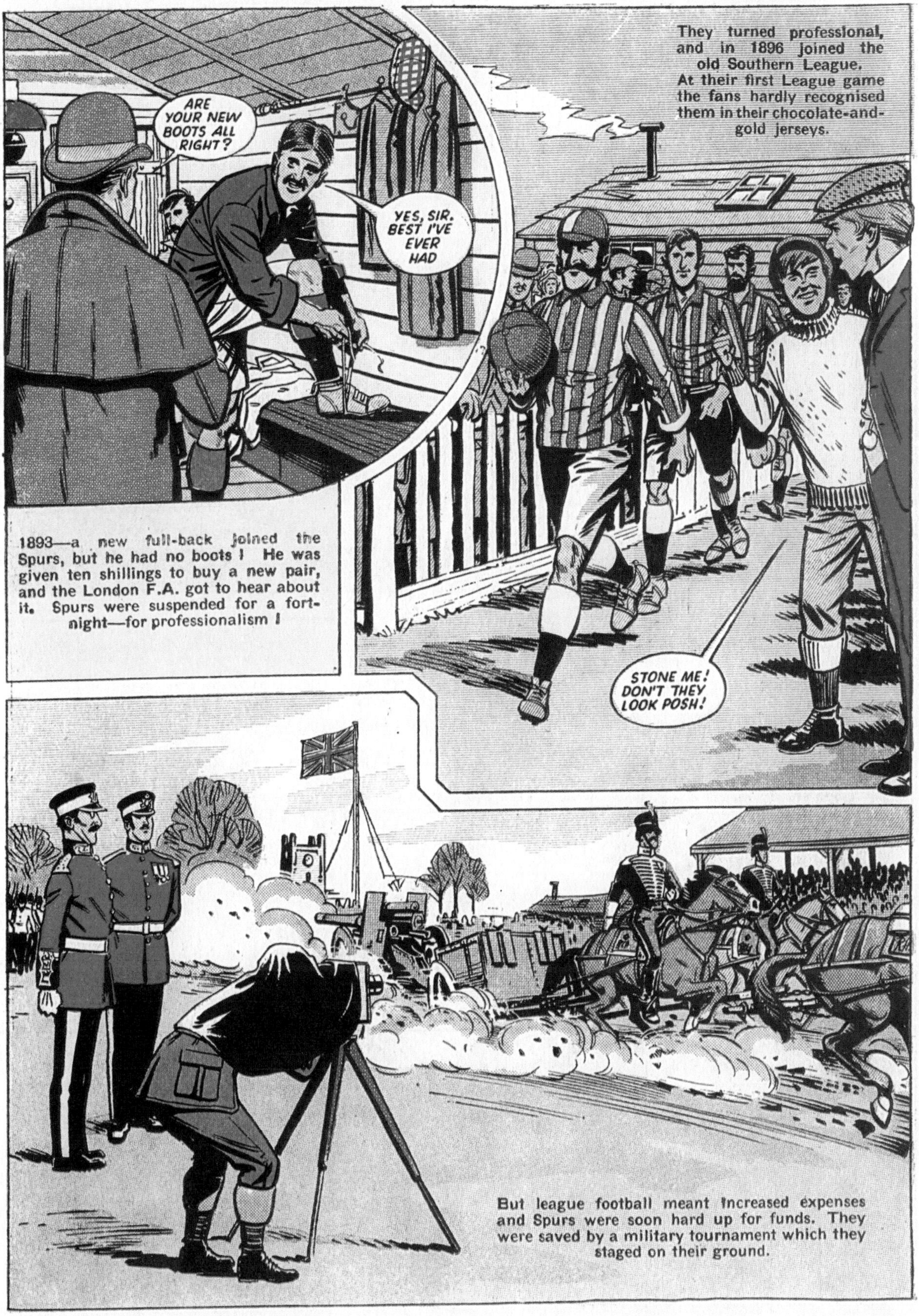
ARE YOUR NEW BOOTS ALL RIGHT?
YES, SIR. BEST I'VE EVER HAD
They turned professional, and in 1896 joined the old Southern League. At their first League game the fans hardly recognised them in their chocolate-and-gold jerseys.
1893—a new full-back joined the Spurs, but he had no boots ! He was given ten shillings to buy a new pair, and the London F.A. got to hear about it. Spurs were suspended for a fortnight—for professionalism !
STONE ME! DON'T THEY LOOK POSH!
But league football meant increased expenses and Spurs were soon hard up for funds. They were saved by a military tournament which they staged on their ground.

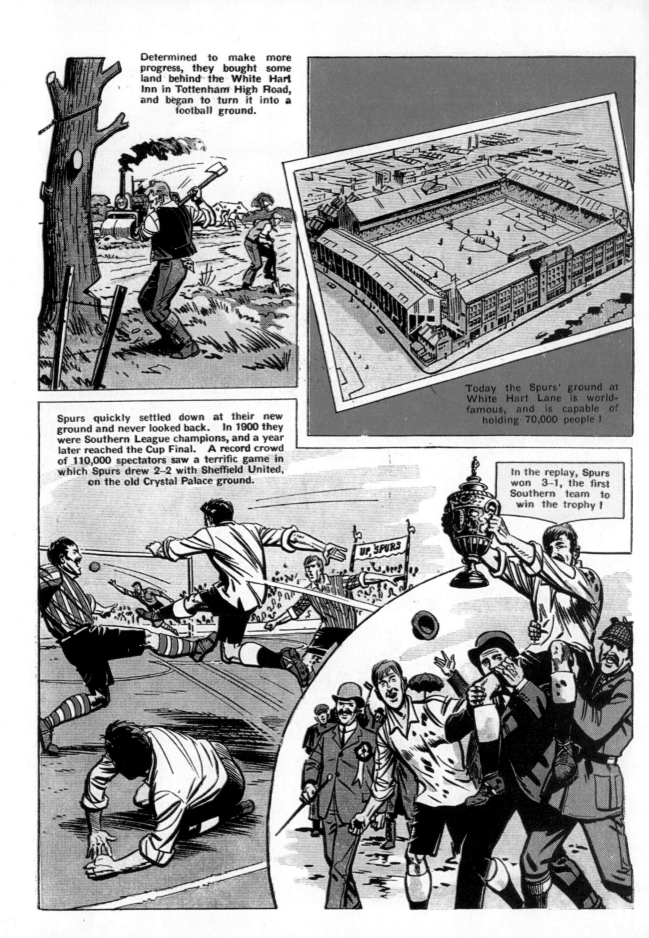

Determined to make more progress, they bought some land behind the White Hart Inn in Tottenham High Road, and began to turn it into a football ground.

Today the Spurs' ground at White Hart Lane is world-famous, and is capable of holding 70,000 people!

Spurs quickly settled down at their new ground and never looked back. In 1900 they were Southern League champions, and a year later reached the Cup Final. A record crowd of 110,000 spectators saw a terrific game in which Spurs drew 2–2 with Sheffield United, on the old Crystal Palace ground.

In the replay, Spurs won 3–1, the first Southern team to win the trophy!

UP, SPURS

On promotion to Division One, an old player made a copper rooster which was erected above the main stand.

GREAT NEWS, LADS. WE'VE BEEN ELECTED TO THE LEAGUE!

In 1908 they heard that Stoke was leaving the league, so Spurs applied to take their place in Division Two.

In 1915 they were relegated once again, but that was the end of football until after the war. Most of the Spurs' footballers joined the army and became footsloggers!

BIT DIFFERENT FROM WHITE HART LANE, ISN'T IT?

DON'T TAKE IT SO HARD, TOMMY

In 1920 they were Division Two champions again. They might have won the Cup, too, but in the 4th round they lost 1–0 to Aston Villa—and it was Spurs' brilliant right-back, Tommy Clay, who put through his own goal!

Twelve months later Spurs gained their revenge. They beat Aston Villa in the 4th round of the Cup —and went on to win the trophy.

Another Spurs' player, Jimmy Seed, left the club in 1928 to become captain of Sheffield Wednesday. His brilliant play in two end-of-season games relegated Spurs to Division Two.

WHAT A CRACKING GOAL. WE SHOULD NEVER HAVE LET JIMMY LEAVE SPURS!

In 1936 a young Welsh miner joined Spurs. He was Ronnie Burgess.

HOW WOULD YOU LIKE TO PLAY FOR SPURS?

GOOD OLD SPURS

That Welsh boy became one of the greatest players in the game. After the war he was elected captain of Spurs and in 1950 he led his brilliant team to the Second Division Championship.

Twelve months later Spurs won the League Championship. It was only the second time in history that a team had achieved Division Two and Division One titles in successive seasons.

Spurs nearly recorded a "trophy treble" in 1952, but they were beaten by Blackpool in a sensational semi-final of the Cup.

From then on Spurs' fortunes were mixed until 1957 when the club began to build one of the finest sides ever to wear their colours—a side that has cost £230,000 in transfer fees—and made soccer history in 1961.

BOBBY SMITH

DANNY BLANCHFLOWER

CLIFF JONES

BILL BROWN

DAVE MACKAY

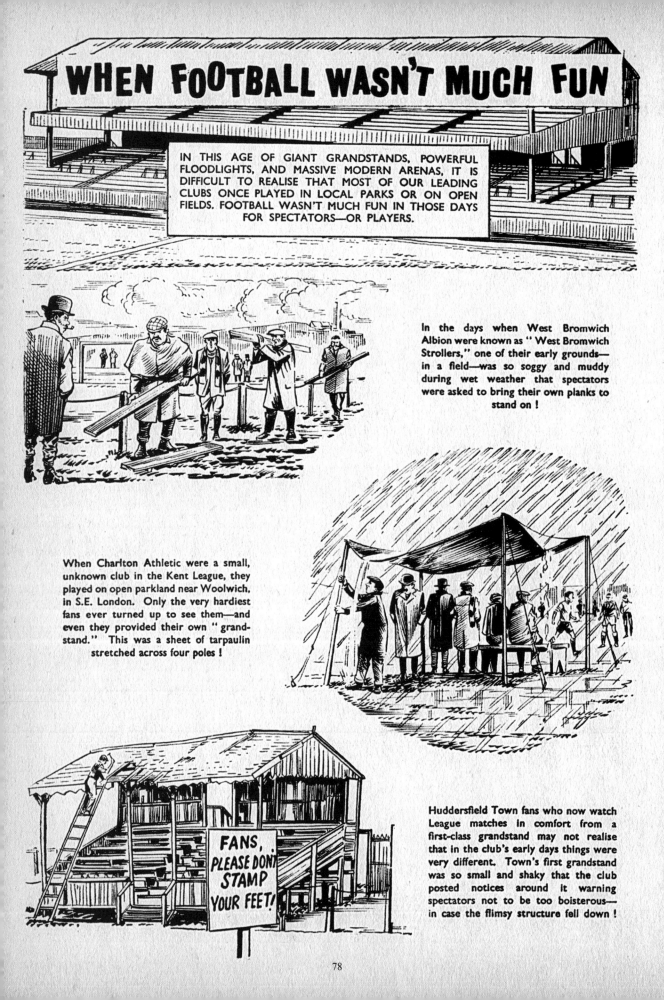

WHEN FOOTBALL WASN'T MUCH FUN

IN THIS AGE OF GIANT GRANDSTANDS, POWERFUL FLOODLIGHTS, AND MASSIVE MODERN ARENAS, IT IS DIFFICULT TO REALISE THAT MOST OF OUR LEADING CLUBS ONCE PLAYED IN LOCAL PARKS OR ON OPEN FIELDS. FOOTBALL WASN'T MUCH FUN IN THOSE DAYS FOR SPECTATORS—OR PLAYERS.

In the days when West Bromwich Albion were known as "West Bromwich Strollers," one of their early grounds—in a field—was so soggy and muddy during wet weather that spectators were asked to bring their own planks to stand on !

When Charlton Athletic were a small, unknown club in the Kent League, they played on open parkland near Woolwich, in S.E. London. Only the very hardiest fans ever turned up to see them—and even they provided their own "grandstand." This was a sheet of tarpaulin stretched across four poles !

FANS, PLEASE DON'T STAMP YOUR FEET!

Huddersfield Town fans who now watch League matches in comfort from a first-class grandstand may not realise that in the club's early days things were very different. Town's first grandstand was so small and shaky that the club posted notices around it warning spectators not to be too boisterous—in case the flimsy structure fell down !

Blackburn Rovers' first ground had a small pond in the centre of the pitch. This was covered over with planks and turf—but one day, during a match, the planks gave way and a player got a ducking!

When Cardiff City were elected to the Southern League more than 50 years ago, they looked around for a ground. In desperation they took over a local refuse dump and after months of hard work by players, officials and supporters, managed to turn it into a football ground. Today that ground—Ninian Park—is one of the finest in Britain, and home of Welsh international matches.

Clapton Orient—now known as Leyton Orient—have had several grounds during the past 80 years. One had a whippet racing track down the side of the pitch. Another had no permanent players' quarters—so an old railway carriage was used as dressing rooms!

Swansea Town's entry into the old Southern League in 1911 was a rush job. So much work had to be done on the ground at Vetch Field (once the home of an amateur side) that men were still completing the erection of the goal-posts when the Swansea and Cardiff players took the field for the first game.

all-action quiz

This notorious buccaneer was the last of the great Sea Wolves. What was he called?
Answer: Captain Teach, alias Blackbeard.

He was the scourge of the Royal Flying Corps in the First World War. Can you name him and the number of Allied planes he shot down.?
Answer: Manfred von Richthofen alias the Red Baron who shot down 80 Allied planes.

You all know the name of the first man on the moon, but who was the second one and the name of the lunar landing craft he used?
Answer: Colonel Edwin J. Aldrin and the craft was Eagle.

When confronted by a shark, how can you scare it away without using any weapon or shark repellent?
Answer: Believe it or not, you shout at it.

Who led the revolt of the gladiators and slaves against the Romans?
Answer: Spartacus.

We've given you some real interesting facts. But with Action Transfers you can make up *your own* exciting adventures. **IT'S SO EASY.**

ADVENTURE! INTRIGUE! ACTION!

From stationers toyshops and newsagents.

Letraset **ACTION TRANSFERS**

2/- EACH

Invasion No. 1 ACTION TRANSFERS LOTS OF RUB DOWN TRANSFERS INSIDE

All you have to do is rub down the colour transfers with a ballpoint pen or pencil on the big full colour background you get in every Action Transfer pack. You position the transfers where you want them to go.

Pirates . . . Moon expedition . . . Roman Gladiators . . . War in the Air . . . Underwater City. These are just some of the Action Transfer Sets you can buy. There's over 35 in the series.

IT'S GREAT FUN
- Action Transfers ONLY 2/- each.
- Super Action Transfers 6/- each.

*Distributed in the U.K. by the Royal Sovereign Pencil Co. Ltd.

THE STORY OF THE F.A. CUP

In 1871, officers of the Football Association decided to start a knock-out contest for a trophy. They met in a room close to St. Paul's Cathedral in London and before they parted they had inaugurated the " F.A. Challenge Cup ".

▲ Fifteen clubs agreed to enter the first Cup competition and each paid £1 towards the purchase of a silver trophy, which cost £20. Then early in 1872 the first Cup draw was made— from the top hat of one of the officials! Only twelve names went "into the hat": the other three original entrants could not afford the 5s. entry fee and dropped out.

▲ Most games were played at the Oval, home of the Surrey cricketers. It was here, too, that the final was played in March 1872 and the Wanderers beat Royal Engineers 1-0. Players wore their ordinary boots: the goals had rope instead of crossbars; there was no referee and no field markings, and only a few hundred fans saw the game.

Sixteen teams entered the second Cup competition. Queen's Park (Glasgow) were given a bye to the semi-finals, but they scratched. They couldn't raise the fare to London! Wanderers met Oxford University in the Final, and won for the second year. The game was played at Lillie Bridge, on the banks of the Thames, with a morning kick-off, so the fans could see the Boat Race later that day.

▼

▲

From then on more and more clubs entered the F.A. Cup competition, although quite a number scratched before they could play any games. Scottish clubs, apart from Queen's Park, soon dropped out. On one occasion Partick Thistle met Cliftonville, in Belfast, and won 11-0—but neither side ever competed again in the " English Cup ".

Some amazing things happened in those early days of the Cup. On one occasion Sheffield and Shropshire Wanderers played two drawn games, but as neither team wanted a third meeting, the two captains tossed for it, and Sheffield won. That was before the days of Sheffield Wednesday and Sheffield United.

▼

▲

Goals were plentiful in many of those old-time Cup games, especially in the earlier rounds when the " giants " of the game were paired with the " unknowns ". Double-figure scores happened quite often, but the record was set up in 1887 when Preston North End, one of the " greats ", beat Hyde 26-0!

In 1895 the F.A. Cup vanished! Aston Villa had won the trophy by beating West Bromwich Albion and were so proud of it that they placed it on view in the shop window of a Birmingham trader. But one dark night a smash and grab raider stole the Cup, and although a reward was offered it was never seen again.

▼

▲

In the same year as Preston North End beat Hyde 26-0 they reached the semi-finals and met West Bromwich Albion at Nottingham. The Albion took the field with only 10 men, because their goalie had not turned up. But soon after the kick-off the goalie, Bob Roberts, suddenly appeared among the crowd and took up his place in goal. He had been held up on the railway. Preston were beaten 1-3.

The story of the Cup is packed with strange incidents that could not happen today. For instance, on one occasion West Bromwich Albion were drawn to play against The Druids, a Welsh amateur team from Wrexham way. But the Welsh team failed to turn up, so the referee ordered Albion to kick off. Within a few seconds they scored—well, there was no one to stop them!—and that was the finish. Victory for Albion!

▼

▲

The second F.A. Cup did not last many seasons—fifteen in all, and then it was presented to Lord Kinnaird, to mark his 21 years as President of the F.A. The red-bearded giant had previously played in 9 finals and gained 5 winner's medals with the Wanderers and Old Etonians. He could play anywhere—he even kept goal in the 1877 final.

Aston Villa and Preston once turned up to play a semi-final at Perry Barr, Birmingham—and 30,000 fans turned up, too. Now the ground held only about 20,000, so it wasn't long before the pitch was invaded. There might have been no game that day had it not been for a couple of soldiers who borrowed cab-horses and used them to clear the ground.

Just about the strangest Cup story of all happened 1915. Bradford City and Norwich City had drawn twic It was wartime and the second replay was arranged fe Lincoln City's ground—but it had to be played behin locked gates! But before half-time several hundre spectators had scrambled over the gates to see Brad ford City win 2-0.

Can you imagine the scene in the Burnley dressing room before the 1924 semi-final against Aston Villa at Bramall Lane, Sheffield? During the morning several of the Burnley chaps caught a bad attack of flu and the doctor said they were not to play—but there were no reserves, so out they had to go. They played like heroes, but Villa won 3-0.

Shocks in 1957 when the Wolves, playing on their own ground at Molineux, were knocked out by Bourne mouth, a Third Division side. Outside-left Reg Cutle scored the only goal of that amazing game—and when h did so he crashed into the goalpost. Down came th whole goal and the game was held up for some minutes There's nothing like the F.A. Cup for thrills—and shocks

The Man with all the Honours
BILLY WRIGHT

1949—WON F.A. CUP AND GOLD WINNER'S MEDAL (ON LEFT), AS CAPTAIN OF WOLVES. NEARLY 100 ENGLISH INTERNATIONAL CAPS (ABOVE)—AN ALL-TIME RECORD.

1952—WON FOOTBALLER OF THE YEAR TROPHY (LEFT). 1954 AND 1958—SKIPPERED WOLVES TO THE LEAGUE CHAMPIONSHIP (RIGHT).

MEET *the* ROVERS' MANAGER

BEN GALLOWAY, CHIEF OF MELCHESTER ROVERS, LETS YOU INTO A FEW SECRETS OF HIS LIFE AS MANAGER OF A BIG LEAGUE CLUB

DON'T LET ROY OVERDO IT, TAFF! HE'D TRAIN ALL DAY IF HE HAD HIS WAY!

MANAGING A FIRST DIVISION CLUB KEEPS ME BUSY SEVEN DAYS A WEEK. I'M USUALLY AT THE GROUND ON WEEKDAYS. BEFORE THE PLAYERS, FOR A BRIEF CONFERENCE WITH MY TRAINER AND COACH REGARDING TRAINING AND INJURY TREATMENT.

THEN THERE'S THE OFFICE WORK TO ATTEND TO—AND BELIEVE ME, THERE'S PLENTY OF THIS! BUT I ALWAYS FIND TIME TO VISIT THE PLAYERS AT THEIR TRAINING. THEY'RE GLAD TO SEE ME, TOO.

MORNING, LADS! GLAD TO SEE YOU'RE IN TOP FORM!

THE MANAGER MAY BE "THE GUV'NOR," BUT HE MUST BE A PAL TO ALL HIS PLAYERS. IF ONE OF THE LADS HAS A PROBLEM, HE KNOWS HE CAN COME INTO THE OFFICE AND TALK IT OVER. THAT'S WHY THE ROVERS HAVE SUCH A HAPPY TEAM SPIRIT.

INJURIES ARE A HEADACHE TO ALL MANAGERS, SO AT LEAST ONCE A WEEK I HAVE A CONFERENCE WITH THE CLUB DOCTOR TO HEAR HIS REPORT ON MY PLAYERS WHO ARE OUT OF ACTION.

I'M AFRAID JACK'S BROKEN HIS WRIST, MR. GALLOWAY

THAT'S TOUGH LUCK, JACKY!

I'M BUSY IN THE EVENINGS, TOO. TWICE A WEEK I REMAIN AT THE STADIUM TO LOOK AT THE JUNIORS. ALTHOUGH I HAVE FULL CONFIDENCE IN MY COACHES, THE LADS LIKE ME TO SHOW AN INTEREST IN THEIR WORK.

I SUGGEST THE SAME FIRST TEAM AS LAST WEEK, GENTLEMEN!

LIKE THE BOSS OF ANY BUSINESS, I AM EXPECTED TO KNOW ALL THAT'S GOING ON IN THE CLUB, SO THAT I CAN ANSWER QUESTIONS AT THE WEEKLY BOARD MEETING. IT IS THERE THAT I ANNOUNCE MY TEAM SELECTIONS FOR THE NEXT GAMES, AND SETTLE ANY OTHER IMPORTANT MATTERS.

THANKS A LOT, MR. GALLOWAY!

ONE OF MY FIRST JOBS AFTER THE BOARD MEETING IS TO ANSWER A CALL FROM THE SPORTS EDITOR OF THE LOCAL PAPER, TO GIVE HIM THE LATEST NEWS OF THE ROVERS.

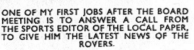

I HAVE TO KEEP IN CLOSE CONTACT WITH THE ROVERS' SCOUTS. WHEN ONE OF THESE OLD PLAYERS RECOMMENDS A PROMISING JUNIOR HE HAS SPOTTED, I USUALLY MEET HIM SO THAT WE CAN WATCH THE LAD IN ACTION.

THAT'S THE LAD I TOLD YOU ABOUT — AT INSIDE-RIGHT

BUT SPOTTING FUTURE STARS HAS ITS HEADACHES. I ONCE DROVE 120 MILES TO WATCH A JUNIOR—BUT HE WASN'T PLAYING! ON THE RETURN JOURNEY MY CAR BROKE DOWN —MILES FROM THE NEAREST 'PHONE! I ARRIVED HOME NEXT MORNING—AFTER A COMPLETELY WASTED JOURNEY!

ANOTHER JOURNEY WAS MORE SUCCESSFUL. I MADE A RUSH-TRIP UP NORTH TO SIGN ON A PROMISING YOUNG FULL-BACK AT THE PIT-HEAD WHERE HE WORKED. HE'S NOW OUR REGULAR RIGHT-BACK, DAVE WILLIAMS.

WE HAVE WITH US TO-NIGHT THE FAMOUS MANAGER OF MELCHESTER ROVERS—MR. BEN GALLOWAY—

I GET PLENTY OF FUN OUT OF MY LIFE, AND RECEIVE MANY INVITATIONS TO SPEAK AT LOCAL SPORTS CLUBS. RECENTLY, TOO, I APPEARED ON TELEVISION, DISCUSSING FOOTBALL WITH OTHER MANAGERS.

ANOTHER OF MY PLEASANT DUTIES IS TO ENTERTAIN THE MANAGER, DIRECTORS AND FRIENDS OF TEAMS VISITING MELCHESTER. IT'S ALWAYS A DELIGHT TO MEET AND CHAT WITH OLD FRIENDS.

GLAD TO SEE THE ROVERS ARE DOING SO WELL, BEN!

THANKS! I'VE GOT A GRAND BUNCH OF LADS!

LOOK OUT, ROY! WATCH THAT HALF-BACK—!

PERHAPS THE MOST EXHAUSTING 90 MINUTES OF ANY WEEK IS WATCHING ROY AND CO. PLAYING A TOUGH LEAGUE OR CUP MATCH. I OFTEN WISH I COULD BE OUT THERE WITH THEM, THEN I MIGHT NOT GET SO EXCITED AND ANXIOUS! BUT I WOULDN'T CHANGE MY LIFE. THE ROVERS ARE A GREAT CLUB, AND I'M PROUD TO BE THEIR MANAGER.

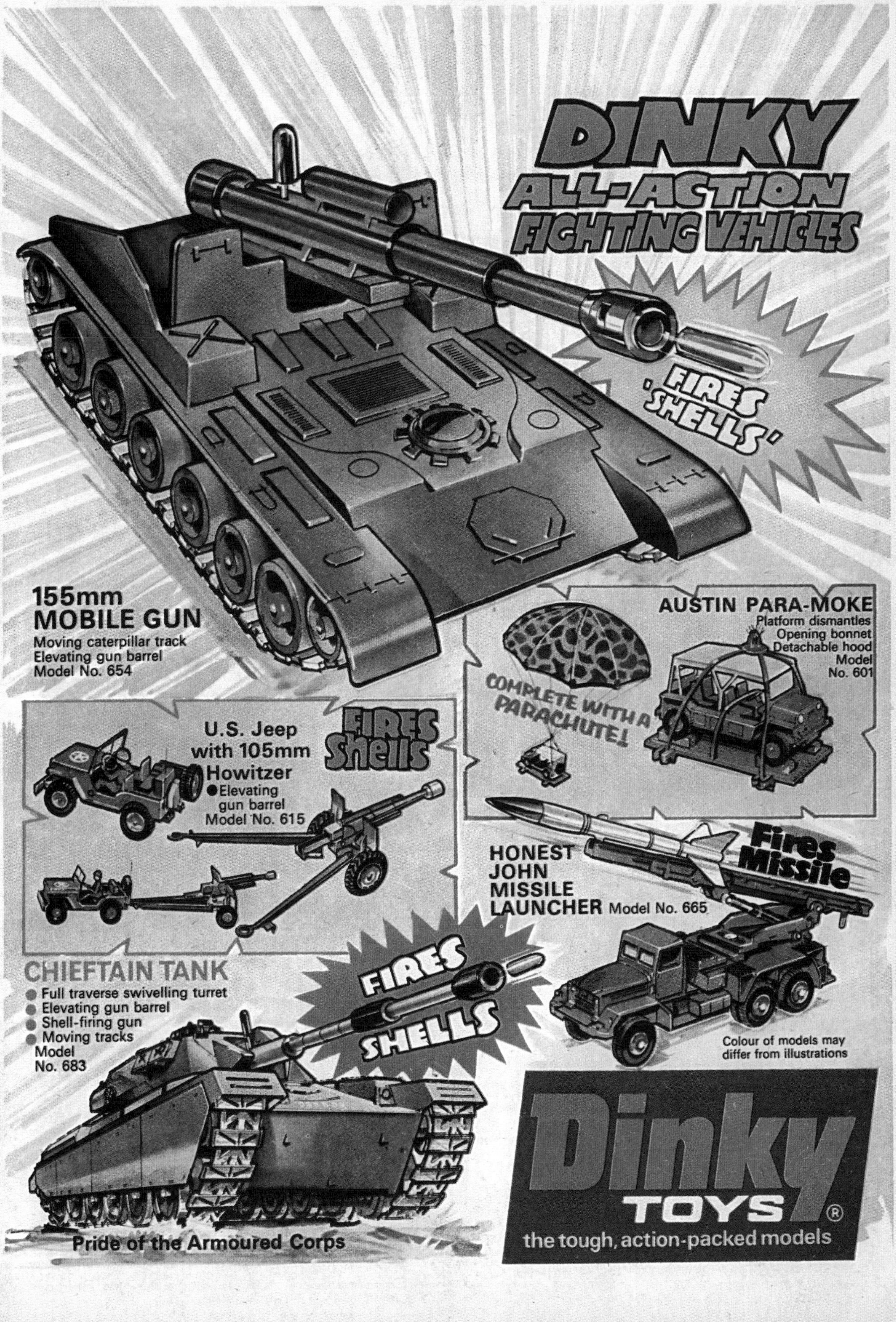
DINKY
ALL-ACTION
FIGHTING VEHICLES
FIRES 'SHELLS'
155mm
MOBILE GUN
Moving caterpillar track
Elevating gun barrel
Model No. 654
AUSTIN PARA-MOKE
Platform dismantles
Opening bonnet
Detachable hood
Model
No. 601
COMPLETE WITH A PARACHUTE!
U.S. Jeep
with 105mm
Howitzer
●Elevating
gun barrel
Model No. 615
FIRES Shells
HONEST
JOHN
MISSILE
LAUNCHER Model No. 665
Fires Missile
CHIEFTAIN TANK
● Full traverse swivelling turret
● Elevating gun barrel
● Shell-firing gun
● Moving tracks
Model
No. 683
FIRES SHELLS
Colour of models may
differ from illustrations
Pride of the Armoured Corps
Dinky
TOYS®
the tough, action-packed models

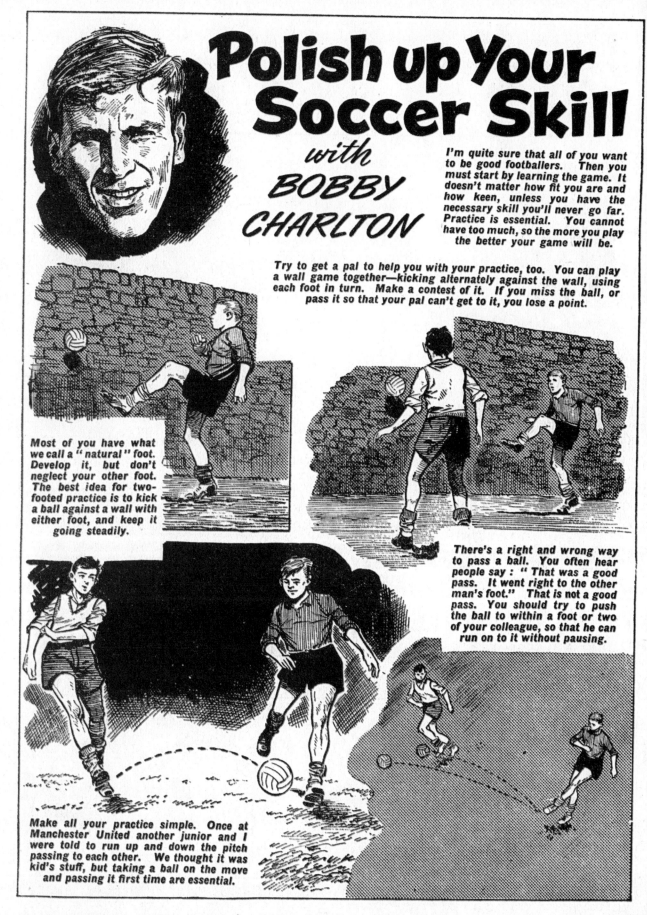

Polish up Your Soccer Skill

with BOBBY CHARLTON

I'm quite sure that all of you want to be good footballers. Then you must start by learning the game. It doesn't matter how fit you are and how keen, unless you have the necessary skill you'll never go far. Practice is essential. You cannot have too much, so the more you play the better your game will be.

Try to get a pal to help you with your practice, too. You can play a wall game together—kicking alternately against the wall, using each foot in turn. Make a contest of it. If you miss the ball, or pass it so that your pal can't get to it, you lose a point.

Most of you have what we call a "natural" foot. Develop it, but don't neglect your other foot. The best idea for two-footed practice is to kick a ball against a wall with either foot, and keep it going steadily.

There's a right and wrong way to pass a ball. You often hear people say : " That was a good pass. It went right to the other man's foot." That is not a good pass. You should try to push the ball to within a foot or two of your colleague, so that he can run on to it without pausing.

Make all your practice simple. Once at Manchester United another junior and I were told to run up and down the pitch passing to each other. We thought it was kid's stuff, but taking a ball on the move and passing it first time are essential.

The ball won't always reach you along the ground, so you must learn to trap it quickly and get it under almost instant control. If it's a dropping ball you can trap it as it touches the ground.

Another means of trapping is with the inside of the foot. As the ball drops, take it with the foot turned slightly inwards and downwards. The body is bent slightly forward so that you can make a quick getaway the moment the ball is under control.

If the ball has bounced in front of you, use the sole of the boot to pull it down.

Lastly, if the ball is dropping fairly fast towards you, trap it on the chest and allow it to drop to your feet. Keep your stomach well tucked-in, though.

Or you can catch the ball on the instep and lower it to the ground. The foot must be moving downwards, otherwise the ball may bounce away and ruin your chance of getting it under control.

If you're a forward, then shoot on sight. In other words, when you see the chance of a shot at goal, take it and don't hesitate. Don't be greedy, of course, and think you're the only sharpshooter in the team. But if your pals work hard and give you the ball, have a go! You won't always score, but better to shoot and miss than not to shoot at all.

For power in your shooting you should get your standing leg alongside the ball, and as you swing forward with your kicking leg, keep your body right over the ball. Foot meets ball, and the leg follows through naturally.

One of the big faults I notice among juniors is that so many of them hold on to the ball too long and then are caught in possession. I'm not suggesting that you kick the ball away the moment you get it, but if you are tackled with the ball you're likely to lose it, so the moment you see a team-mate in position for a pass, let him have it. Then get ready for a return pass.

Heading is important and demands concentrated practice. The correct way to head a ball is to take it on the top of the forehead (not the top of the head!) and nod it in the direction you want it to go. Get a pal to join you for a spell of heading practice. Stand a few yards apart and nod the ball backwards and forwards to each other, varying the height and speed as much as possible.

My remarks about heading the ball to a colleague don't apply in front of goal, of course. When that happens you must act quickly. Leap to the ball, take it on the front of the forehead and either nod it straight down into the net or, with a quick flick of the neck, send it flashing past the goalie.

Every player should know how to take a throw-in. It's usually the job of the wing-half, but often a throw by another member of the side can set up an attack. Remember, the ball must be thrown from behind the head, two-handed, and part of both feet must be on or behind the touchline. Try always to throw to a colleague clear of opposition. Remember, a throw-in can be as valuable as a free-kick.

Now let me finish with a few general tips. If you asked what helped me most when I first joined Manchester United I'd say it was the advice I was given by older and more experienced men. Any young player who thinks he knows it all won't get far, so ask for advice—and take it. I did, and I've never regretted it. Nothing can be more valuable than advice from your elders.

Never forget that football is a team game, so don't start growling if you're picked to play in a position that isn't "your own." Give of your best wherever you're put. I always thought inside-left was my best position, but I've since played for England in four different positions. Nowadays I'm willing to play anywhere—even in goal if they want me there.

Here's wishing you the best of luck in your football. Play fairly and play to win. I'm sure you'll enjoy it!

75 Big Prizes in WAYFINDERS Tracking Competition

Easy to win! Fun to enter! You get five chances for a prize when you choose Wayfinders!

25 1st PRIZES ELSWICK HOPPER CYCLES

50 OTHER PRIZES SCALEXTRIC RACING SETS

WAYFINDERS the adventure shoe

A HIPPO B WOLF C BUFFALO
D ZEBRA E RHINO F TIGER

HERE'S HOW TO ENTER

You just match up the animals shown at left with their tracks. For example, if you think track 4 is that of Tiger 'F', insert 4 in box opposite F . . . and do the same until all animals are paired up. Then complete the sentence below, using not more than ten words. YOU ARE ALLOWED UP TO FIVE TRIES PER ENTRY . . . SO YOU HAVE FIVE CHANCES TO WIN!

Post your completed entry along with shoe illustration from Green Guarantee Slip found in Wayfinders box to : Wayfinders Competition, 18-20 St. Andrew St., London E.C 4. (Comp.)

	TRY 1	TRY 2	TRY 3	TRY 4	TRY 5
A					
B					
C					
D					
E					
F					

NAME
BLOCK CAPITALS
ADDRESS

AGE SHOE SIZE

I LIKE MY WAYFINDERS BECAUSE

PLEASE CUT OUT

Entries valid only on purchases during contest period.   TH/2

HAVE A SHOT AT THIS

The Solution will be
found on page 117.

SOCCER CROSSWORD PUZZLE

CLUES

ACROSS

1. Famous First Division club.
5. " Much — About Nothing."
6. Nationality of McParland (Aston Villa).
9. Rovers' centre-forward.
11. The Cup Final takes place there.
12. Peter Broadbent (initials).
14. Two of them make up one.
15. This would have studs if it was used for Soccer.
17. George Lee (initials).
20. A regulation.
22. To be in debt.
24. Port Vale inside-forward.
25. A ball kicked before it bounces.
26. You can hear it at Hampden Park sometimes.
27. Soccer is one — and so is tennis.
28. To compete with.
31. Leyton Orient (initials).
33. Difficult to kick (two words).
35. Bristol City forward.
38. To defeat.
40. Famous Scottish League team.
42. Footballer might keep his kit in one.
43. Some of the early Cup Finals were played there.
44. Famous London club (two words).
46. Schemes.
47. They play at Brisbane Road, London.
49. First and last letters of " Birmingham City."
50. London Transport (initials).
51. Some bowlers can make the ball do this.
53. A plan.
55. Eric Moore (initials).
58. First two letters of " Everton."
59. Fulham play — Craven Cottage.
60. A poem.
61. Roy Race usually makes the most of them.
64. ——— Rovers are a famous Scottish team.
66. You go through one on your way out from a football ground.
68. Almost a duet.
69. Well-known football club from South London.
70. An enemy.
71. Perceived.
72. East Fife (initials).

DOWN

1. Not high.
2. The referee blows his whistle for it.
3. It goes with a sceptre.
4. Nought.
5. A Scottish team.
7. You would find one at the Zoo.
8. First and last letters of " Hull City."
9. An old piece of cloth.
10. Used for lubricating.
12. The Speedway Pirates ride there.
13. Nobody does this in a footer match.
16. Middlesbro's on this river.
18. Sometimes put down on turf to protect it from frost.
19. An event in the Olympic Games.
20. You'd never see him on the football field, but he's a very famous cyclist (two words).
21. Opposite of " morn."
23. A goalie's job.
24. Stirling Albion (initials).
26. No club likes to be ——————.
29. Roy and Blackie are ———.
30. Lawton's first name.
32. Oldham Athletic (initials).
34. Tennis is sometimes played on them.
36. A kind of mascot.
37. It might be a cry of derision.
38. You can't play without one.
39. An action made immediately before a match starts.
41. " A " is one, and so is " B."
42. Bill Perry (initials).
45. Most players enjoy this after a game (two words).
48. You have to use them, if you want to shoot accurately.
52. You can read all about the big matches in them.
54. To avoid.
56. Part of a net.
57. The Villa come from this place.
59. Past tense of " eat."
62. Wheels revolve on it.
63. A place or situation.
65. Would be an I.O.U. if it had an " O."
67. Not on.

100 YEARS OF FOOTBALL "FASHIONS"

See How the Soccer Stars' Dress has Changed

When Queen's Park (Glasgow) were formed nearly 100 years ago, the players paid little attention to dress. In fact, they wore their ordinary clothes, with only a "Q.P." armband to distinguish them from their opponents!

Some teams sported distinctive coloured caps—Nottingham Forest wore red flannel; Blackburn Rovers blue and white; and Luton blue and pink. That's why a cap became the first award for international selection.

THEN . . .
This is how the old-time footballer dressed. It's the red-bearded Hon. A. F. Kinnaird, who appeared in 9 Finals and won 5 Cup medals in the early days. Yes, he played in that quartered cap, long white trousers and his ordinary boots!

To-day, players prize their caps so highly that they are seldom seen, but goalie Bob Roberts, the first West Bromwich Albion footballer to play for England (1887), was so proud of his cap—and his white shirt—that he always wore them in League and Cup games! He also played in long white trousers!

The earliest "shorts" were, in fact, "longs". In 1904, the F.A. decreed that "knickerbockers should cover the knees". The following season, several players were fined for breaking this rule, including Herbert Smith, of Reading (left), who was picked for England. But that curious rule was soon withdrawn

Samuel Weller Widdowson (above) a Nottingham Forest and England stalwart, invented shinguards in 1874, because hacking was general in his day. But at first, most players wore them OUTSIDE their stockings, as did Charlie Athersmith (below), who, in 1896–7, won 3 international caps, and Cup and League Championship medals with Aston Villa—a wonderful record

For many years the goalkeeper wore the same coloured shirt as the rest of his team-mates. Here's Willie Foulke, who weighed 20 stone, wearing Sheffield United's red and white stripes. Then in 1909, the F.A. made a rule that the goalie's jersey should be of a different colour from either of the competing teams

. . . NOW

So we come to the player of to-day with his short-sleeved, collarless and numbered shirt; brief, tailor-made shorts; bright stockings; slim shinguards and lightweight boots. This new-style reflects the Continental influence on British Soccer. It's certainly smarter than the old-time dress, isn't it?

Colours of FAMOUS

SPARTAK
★ RUSSIA

JUVENTUS
★ ITALY

HONVED
★ HUNGARY

REAL MADRID
★ SPAIN

MOSCOW DYNAMOS
★ RUSSIA

OVERSEAS CLUBS

RAPID
* AUSTRIA

BARCELONA
* SPAIN

BORUSSIA
* GERMANY

RIVER PLATE
* ARGENTINE

NICE
* FRANCE

LEAGUE CLUB BADGES

THE RANGERS

BOLTON WANDERERS

HEART OF MIDLOTHIAN

NOTTS COUNTY

ASTON VILLA

EVERTON

PARTICK THISTLE

MIDDLESBROUGH

DUNDEE

CHARLTON

MILLWALL

LIVERPOOL

BADGES WORN by WORLD CUP TEAMS

YUGOSLAVIA

THE WORLD CUP

SWITZERLAND

BRAZIL

ISRAEL

FRANCE

ITALY

BELGIUM

SWEDEN

AUSTRIA

THEY MUST HAVE THEIR MASCOTS!

BLACKPOOL'S FAMOUS DUCK MASCOT IS NOW WELL KNOWN ALL OVER THE COUNTRY. IT TRAVELS TO ALL THE TEAM'S BIG MATCHES.

NEWCASTLE UNITED ARE KNOWN AS "THE MAGPIES"—AND THEY'RE PROUD OF THEIR LATEST MASCOT, A MAGPIE IN A GLASS CASE.

WEST BROMWICH ALBION KEEP THEIR MASCOT IN A CAGE. IT'S A TAME THRUSH (OR THROSTLE), BUT THEN ALBION ARE ALWAYS KNOWN AS "THE THROSTLES."

THIS STUFFED COCKEREL IS ALWAYS WELL IN EVIDENCE AT WHITE HART LANE, HOME OF THE FAMOUS SPURS.

HERE'S ROY WITH BILLY THE GOAT, THE POPULAR MASCOT OF MEL-CHESTER ROVERS.

KEEP FIT *for* FOOTER

1. Weight-lifting is now an essential part of the training programme of most first-class football teams, because it has been proved so beneficial for muscle strengthening. It can help YOU, too. No need to worry if you can't afford the correct apparatus. You can make your own weights with a strong pole and a couple of buckets. Pour a little water in each bucket to start with, and then increase it after every few lifts. For individual wrist lifts, you can use old flat-irons. But don't strain yourself.

2. Here's an exercise that will toughen up your stomach and thigh muscles. Sit on the floor, legs stretched out in front of you, and get a pal to hold them down firmly by the ankles. Now, hands on hips, stretch slowly backwards until your shoulders touch the floor. Raise up slowly, keeping your stomach muscles tensed. Do this about half a dozen times, but no more. Remember, overdoing any exercise can be harmful. You can so easily strain yourself!

3. This looks like jolly good fun—and so it is, but it's good training, too. Leg, arm, back, stomach and neck muscles will all benefit from this exercise, providing you take it seriously. Four of you squat on the floor, legs stretched out in front of you so that all your feet are touching in the centre. Grip hands, and bend backwards until your arms are at full stretch. Hold it for a moment. Now, at the word " Go ", the two lads sitting " North and South " press hard with the feet and pull on the arms. That will force your pals sitting " East and West " to strain against the force of your pull. But the idea of this exercise is not to see which pair is the stronger. The pulling of the alternate pairs must be in rhythm—pull, give, pull, give, and so on. If you do this properly, about fifty times, you'll have had enough and feel fagged. That's the time to stop. But do take it seriously!

4. Cycling is one of the best of all training sports, but " cycling without a bike " is even more beneficial. I expect you've done it many times, but do you do it correctly? You must get your legs and body well up on your elbows, so that you can feel the pull across your top back and neck muscles. When you start " pedalling " in the air, bring your knees well back into your body each time and really kick at full stretch. Start slowly and work up your speed, as you would on a real bike. But be warned once more—as soon as you feel an ache anywhere, pack it up!

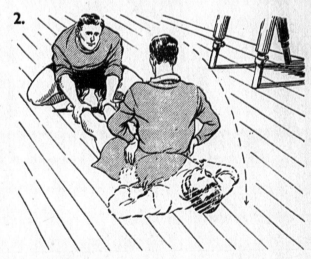

ROY'S SOCCER QUIZ

Have a shot at solving these 12 football posers before you turn to the answers on page 159. Award yourself 2 points for each correct answer. If you score 18 or over, you can give yourself a pat on the back. Try them out on your pals, too.

Can a football pitch be completely square, providing the length and the width come within the F.A. regulation dimensions?

Newcastle United are the only club to win the F.A. Cup three times since the War. How many players appeared in all three finals?

A Football League game starts with a dark-coloured ball, but after an hour's play, the light becomes so bad that the ref. calls for a white ball. Is he right or wrong?

What is the biggest aggregate of goals in a Football League match—and how many did each side score?

Where is the largest football ground in Britain—which club plays there—and what is the record attendance?

Which club has won the League Championship most times—Sunderland, Newcastle, Arsenal or Manchester United ?

When was the first penalty awarded in a Wembley Cup Final—1925, 1930, 1938 or 1948—and who took it ?

Who was the first player to be transferred for a fee of £30,000 or more ?

In which Soccer Competition is the " Jules Rimet Cup " presented to the winners ?

Who was the first man to become " Footballer of the Year " twice ?

Has a player ever kept goal in a Cup Final wearing spectacles ?

Which club won promotion from the Third Division (South) to the First Division in two successive seasons—and when was it ?

The " old " Wembley (1923) . . .

WONDERFUL WEMBLEY

WEMBLEY—there is magic in the name, for the Empire Stadium is one of the world's greatest sports arenas. Built in 1923 at a cost of £750,000, with accommodation for more than 100,000 spectators, it has become the " home " of English football. In 1963 the Stadium was completely roofed in, making it the largest covered sports arena in Britain.

. . . and the " new " (1963).

The FIRST CUP FINAL

It happened in 1923. Nearly 200,000 turned up to see West Ham play Bolton Wanderers. Gates were broken down, spectators invaded the pitch (top picture), and there was talk of postponing the match. Eventually, mounted police pushed the fans back behind the touchlines so that the game could commence— 40 minutes late. King George V was among those who waited for the kick-off.

In this historic picture the Bolton and West Ham captains are trying to lead their players on to the field through the seething crowds swarming all over the pitch. Several times during the match the fans pressed over the touchlines but Bolton eventually won 2—0.

❋   ❋   ❋

Royalty are always present at the Cup Final. In 1948 King George VI was introduced to the Manchester United team by their skipper Johnny Carey. Later that afternoon His Majesty presented them with the Cup and medals.

A proud moment for the captain when he receives the Cup. Here is Harry Johnston (Blackpool) taking the trophy from Queen Elizabeth in 1953.

Then comes triumphal retur the pitch from Royal Box to thunderous appl of the fans. Slater leads victorious Wolve 1960 after bea Blackburn Ro 3-0.

Lastly—the victors pose for the photographers with the Cup held on high for all to see. This was the scene in 1955 when Jimmy Scoular and his Newcastle United team-mates celebrated their victory over Manchester City.

MEMORABLE MOMENTS

STANLEY MATTHEWS will never forget the day he won his Cup medal (1953) after twice being on the losing side at Wembley. Blackpool's winning goal against Bolton came in the last minute of a sensational Final.

England play Scotland every alternate year at Wembley. In 1961 they won with a record score—9–3. It gave England the International Championship and Skipper Johnny Haynes (Fulham) was chaired off the field by his triumphant team-mates.

Another proud moment for an England skipper. In 1959 Billy Wright (Wolves) not only led England to victory over Scotland, but this was his 100th international appearance, a world record.

History was made at Wembley in October 1963, when England beat the Rest of the World in the F.A. Centenary Match. After the game the England players lined up to applaud their famous opponents.

▲

Penalty! Danny Blanchflower, Spurs captain, scores against Burnley's 'keeper Adam Blacklaw in the 1962 Cup Final.

Goal! Jackie Milburn puts Newcastle United one-up in the first few minutes of the 1955 Cup Final against Manchester City.

▼

▲

Tragedy for Bert Turner, of Charlton Athletic, when he put through his "own goal" in the 1946 Final against Derby County. But a few minutes later he shot the equaliser—the only man to score for BOTH sides at Wembley!

Brazil, World Cup winners, were leading England 1–0 at Wembley (1963) until a few minutes from the end, when Bryan Douglas (Blackburn Rovers) slipped in the equaliser—although he was flat on the turf!

▼

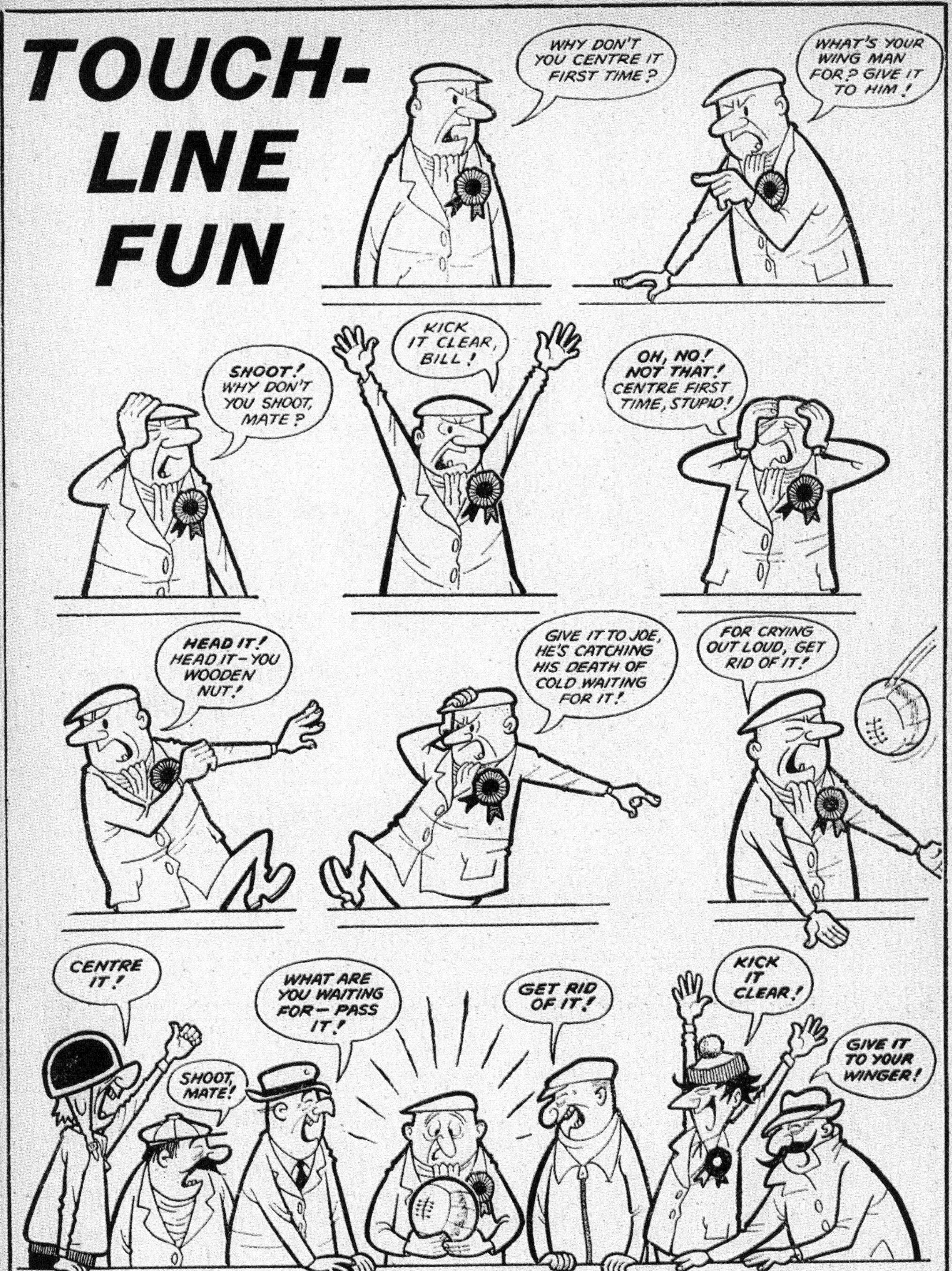
TOUCH-LINE FUN
WHY DON'T YOU CENTRE IT FIRST TIME?
WHAT'S YOUR WING MAN FOR? GIVE IT TO HIM!
SHOOT! WHY DON'T YOU SHOOT, MATE?
KICK IT CLEAR, BILL!
OH, NO! NOT THAT! CENTRE FIRST TIME, STUPID!
HEAD IT! HEAD IT—YOU WOODEN NUT!
GIVE IT TO JOE, HE'S CATCHING HIS DEATH OF COLD WAITING FOR IT!
FOR CRYING OUT LOUD, GET RID OF IT!
CENTRE IT!
SHOOT, MATE!
WHAT ARE YOU WAITING FOR—PASS IT!
GET RID OF IT!
KICK IT CLEAR!
GIVE IT TO YOUR WINGER!

The EARLY DAYS of the Rovers

GATHER ROUND, LADS! ROY'S FATHER TURNS SOME MORE PAGES OF HIS WONDERFUL SCRAP-BOOK OF THE ROVERS' HISTORY FOR YOU.

Here's a picture of the first goal scored by Rovers after their promotion to the First Division. It was banged in by centre-forward "Bullet" Johnson—and how well named he was!

The Melchester Chronicle

ROVERS' SCOTTISH CAPTURE
Jock Cameron Signed for Large Fee

The well known Scottish centre-half, Jock Cameron, has agreed to join the Rovers. We understand the transfer fee was nearly £2,000, but he should prove the player the club need to restore their confidence and pu...

But Rovers struck a bad patch and were soon struggling near the foot of Division I. So they paid a big transfer fee for a famous Scottish centre-half, Jock Cameron. He was a grand footballer, and under his captaincy, Rovers climbed clear of the relegation danger. That's Jock and the team below.

At the end of that season, Rovers went on their first Continental tour. They won all their games by big scores, and gained a fine silver cup (seen above). But they must have been embarrassed when they were presented with bouquets by their opponents before each game!

Next season, misfortune befell the club. During a gale, part of the stand was burned out, and the players lost most of their kit.

Rovers' Three Caps

Steve Wilson Plays for England

All Melchester is proud of the new international honours that have come to the Rovers' players. No doubt there will be many more in the future. Steve Wilson, the ~~Rovers~~ popular goal-keeps

Here's another proud memory of the early Rovers—Taff Morgan (Wales), Jock Cameron (Scotland), and Steve Wilson (England)—all chosen for international honours in the same season. Taff's now Rovers' trainer, of course.

But although Rovers had lost their stand, they made the best of a bad job and carried on—wearing borrowed kit!

Worse was to come, however. Rovers had to leave their ground! Fortunately, they found a new site, but players and fans spent the whole of the close season working feverishly to turn that piece of waste ground into a football pitch.

It was a hectic rush to finish the job, as this picture shows. The workmen were only just completing the erection of the goalposts as the teams took the field for the first match—at Melchester Stadium, now one of the finest grounds in the country!

ROVERS IN THE FINAL!

Jock Cameron's winning goal from Taffy Jones' corner kick. Rovers meet Eastfield Wanderers.

Unfortunately, it was a terribly wet winter. The new turf churned up badly, and several matches had to be abandoned —because the ref. couldn't see which players were which!

But Rovers overcame all their problems. With Jock Cameron an inspiring skipper, they did so well in the Cup that they reached the Final for the first time in their history! What a proud day that was for Melchester!

MORE EXCITING PAGES FROM MR. RACE'S BOOK OF MEMORIES WILL COME LATER.

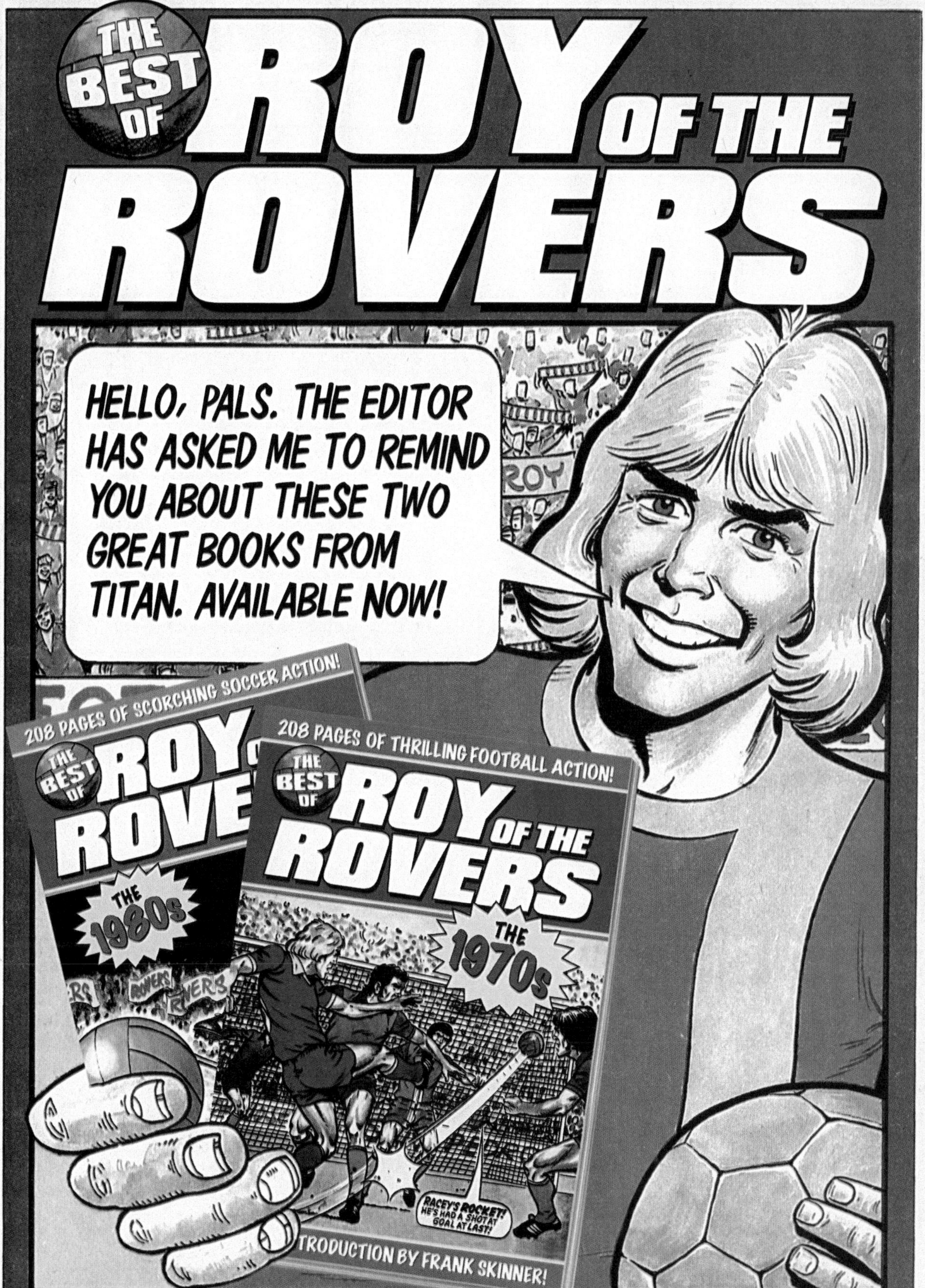
THE BEST OF ROY OF THE ROVERS
HELLO, PALS. THE EDITOR HAS ASKED ME TO REMIND YOU ABOUT THESE TWO GREAT BOOKS FROM TITAN. AVAILABLE NOW!
208 PAGES OF SCORCHING SOCCER ACTION!
THE BEST OF ROY OF THE ROVERS
THE 1980s
208 PAGES OF THRILLING FOOTBALL ACTION!
THE BEST OF ROY OF THE ROVERS
THE 1970s
RACEY'S ROCKET! HE'S HAD A SHOT AT GOAL AT LAST!
TRODUCTION BY FRANK SKINNER!

HOW MANY "POINTS" DID YOU SCORE?

Check up Your Answers to the Quiz and Puzzle Features

IF YOU WERE THE REF

(*See pages* 38 *and* 39)

1. No goal! Law 10 states quite definitely that a goal cannot be scored unless the WHOLE of the ball has passed over the goal-line. In this case, the ball was only ON the line, and not over it.

2. You could not award any type of free-kick. Until the ball is thrown in, it is out of play, and the law concerning free-kicks does not apply. But, of course, you would not allow play to proceed until you had cautioned the offending player, or, if the foul was serious enough, you could order him from the field.

3. There is nothing you could do. Law 1, governing the field of play, states that a flag-post *may* be placed opposite the half-way line on each side of the field, not less than 1 yard outside the touchline. But such flags are NOT essential.

4. This is a clear case of a penalty award against the goalie. Law 12 (according to a decision of the International Board 1956) states that if the goalkeeper pushes an opponent with the ball whilst holding it, the referee shall award a penalty kick for an intentional foul.

5. The ref. was wrong! Law 1 again states that the substitution of the bar by a rope or tape cannot be allowed. In the event of the cross-bar becoming displaced, and there is no avail-able means of replacing it, the match shall be abandoned.

6. No penalty! Law 12 makes it quite clear that the infringement must be INTENTIONAL. The F.A.s advice to referees says: "Unless the hand or arm strikes or propels the ball, it is not a foul. Far too often a player is penalised when the ball touches his arm through no intentional action of his own."

7. The player "8" is NOT offside. Law 11 says: "A player who is not in an offside position when one of his colleagues passes the ball to him, does not become offside if he goes forward during the flight of the ball."

8. No infringement is committed if a second player takes a penalty after a re-kick has been ordered by the referee.

9. The player would be entitled to join the game, even at such a late hour. Law 3 states that "the game shall be played by two teams each consisting of not more than eleven players . . ." Providing he receives the ref.'s permission, the eleventh player can take the field at any time.

10. This is quite O.K. Law 13 covers such an incident by stating: "No player of the opposite side shall approach within 10 yards of the ball . . . UNLESS HE BE STANDING ON HIS OWN GOAL-LINE."

11. This is not a FAIR charge, although it is being made with the shoulder. The player in white has one arm across his opponent's body, thus obstructing him, and the ball is not within playing distance (Law 12).

The Second Bumper Book of Roy of the Rovers
ISBN: 9781848564435
Published by Titan Books, a division of Titan Publishing Group Ltd, 144 Southwark St, London SE1 0UP

First Edition: October 2009
2 4 6 8 10 9 7 5 3 1

This book is just for fun! Football rules are not those of the present day, and items and competitions shown in advertisements may no longer be available.

What did you think of this book? We love to hear from our readers. Please email us at readerfeedback@titanemail.com, or write to us at the above address.
To receive advance information, news, competitions and exclusive Titan offers on-line, please register by clicking the "sign up" button on our website: www.titanbooks.com

Much of the comic strip material used by Titan in this edition is exceedingly rare. As such, we hope that readers appreciate that the quality of the materials can be variable.

A CIP catalogue record for this title is available from the British Library.

This book is dedicated to the unsung heroes of the *Roy of the Rovers* annuals including artists Joe Colquhoun [Stewart Colwyn], Bert Vandeput, Geoff Campion, Paul Trevellion, Colin Page, Fred Holmes, Royman Browne. Writers Frank F. Pepper, Ted Cowan, Tom Tully, Fred Baker and original Roy editor Derek Birnage.

Printed and bound in Italy.

ROY'S SOCCER QUIZ

(*See pages* 104 *and* 105)

1. No. Law 1, concerning the dimensions of the pitch states quite definitely that "the length shall in all cases exceed the breadth."

2. Only three players appeared in all three Newcastle United post-war Cup-winning sides (1951, 1952, 1955)—Bobby Mitchell, Jackie Milburn and Bobby Cowell.

3. The ref. cannot call for a white ball *if* he starts the game with a coloured ball. If, however, a white ball was used at the start, then he can call for a new *white* ball at any time.

4. The highest aggregate of goals in a League match is 17. On Dec. 26, 1935, Tranmere Rovers beat Oldham Athletic (Div. 3, North) 13-4, and the Tranmere centre-forward missed a penalty.

5. The largest ground in Britain is Hampden Park (Glasgow), home of the Queen's Park club. The record attendance at this ground is 149,547, when Scotland met England in April, 1937.

6. Arsenal have won the League Championship 7 times (a record). Aston Villa and Sunderland come next with 6 each.

7. The first penalty awarded in a Wembley Cup Final was in 1938, when George Mutch scored for Preston North End against Huddersfield Town. It was the winning goal in the last minute of extra time.

8. Jackie Sewell. In March, 1951, he was transferred from Notts County to Sheffield Wednesday for a fee of £34,000. He later moved on to Aston Villa.

9. The Jules Rimet Cup is better known as The World Cup. It was first presented to the competition in 1930, by M. Jules Rimet.

10. Tom Finney first won the "Footballer of the Year" trophy in 1954. The Preston North End favourite took the title for the second time in 1957.

11. Yes—in 1922, when J. F. Mitchell kept goal for Preston North End against Huddersfield Town. The latter won 1-0.

12. Charlton Athletic won the Third Division Championship in 1935, and the following season were runners-up in Division 2, and promoted to the First Division.

SOCCER CROSSWORD

(*See pages* 94 *and* 95)

ACROSS: 1. Luton. 5. Ado. 6. Irish. 9. Roy. 11. Wembley. 12. P.B. 14. Pair. 15. Boot. 17. G.L. 20. Rule. 22. Owe. 24. Steele. 25. Volley. 26. Roar. 27. Game. 28. Vie. 31. L.O. 33. Wet ball. 35. Atyeo. 38. Beat. 40. Alloa. 42. Bag. 43. Oval. 44. West Ham. 46. Plans. 47. Orient. 49. B.Y. 50. L.T. 51. Spin. 53. System. 55. E.M. 58. E.V. 59. At. 60. Ode. 61. Passes. 64. Raith. 66. Exit. 68. Due. 69. Charlton. 70. Foe. 71. Seen. 72. E.F.

DOWN: 1. Low. 2. Time. 3. Orb. 4. Nil. 5. Ayr. 7. Seal. 8. HY. 9. Rag. 10. Oil. 12. Poole. 13. Bowl. 16. Tees. 18. Straw. 19. Decathlon. 20. Reg Harris. 21. Eve. 23. Save. 24. S.A. 26. Relegated. 29. Pals. 30. Tommy. 32. O.A. 34. Lawns. 36. Totem. 37. Yah. 38. Ball. 39. Toss. 41. Letter. 42. B.P. 45. A bath. 48. Eyes. 52. Papers. 54. Evade. 56. Mesh. 57. Aston. 59. Ate. 62. Axle. 63. Site. 65. I.U. 67. Off.

HOW TO PLAY OUR FOOTER GAME
(*See coloured pages at the end of this Annual*)

The rules of our Soccer game at the back of this book are quite simple.

Toss-up in the usual way. Winner kicks off with first throw of the dice, and moves the "ball"—(a sixpence will do)—the appropriate number of spaces. Then you and your opponent take alternate throws, unless either of you throws a "6", which gives you a second throw.

Always try to move towards one of your own players. If you throw a number which takes you on to a team-mate, you take another throw, and if that number takes you to another of your own players, then you throw again—and so on. You need not throw the exact number. For instance, if you throw a "5", and can land on a team-mate with "4", then that's O.K., but you don't use the odd one. Simply throw again.

But if you move the ball so that it lands on—or passes OVER—an opponent, you lose possession of the ball, and he carries on.

If a defender lands on the "penalty" spot, it's a penalty for the other side. You can score from the spot with a "3" or more. Likewise with any shot at goal. You need not throw the exact number to take the ball past the goalie. Too few means that the goalie saves. Too many means that the goalie is beaten. Goal!

If you are attacking and land on a "corner" spot, that entitles you to another throw—and often leads to a goal, if you work your moves right and throw the numbers to take the ball to a team-mate.

Decide between yourselves how long you will play—5 or 10 minutes each way should be enough. By the way, the players on the pitch are numbered as in ordinary football—from goal to outside-left, so that you can work out real Soccer moves.

After a few games, you should soon become quite expert in your moves, then you can pick your own teams and start a league. It'll give you hours of fun and good sport. So off you go—shoot!

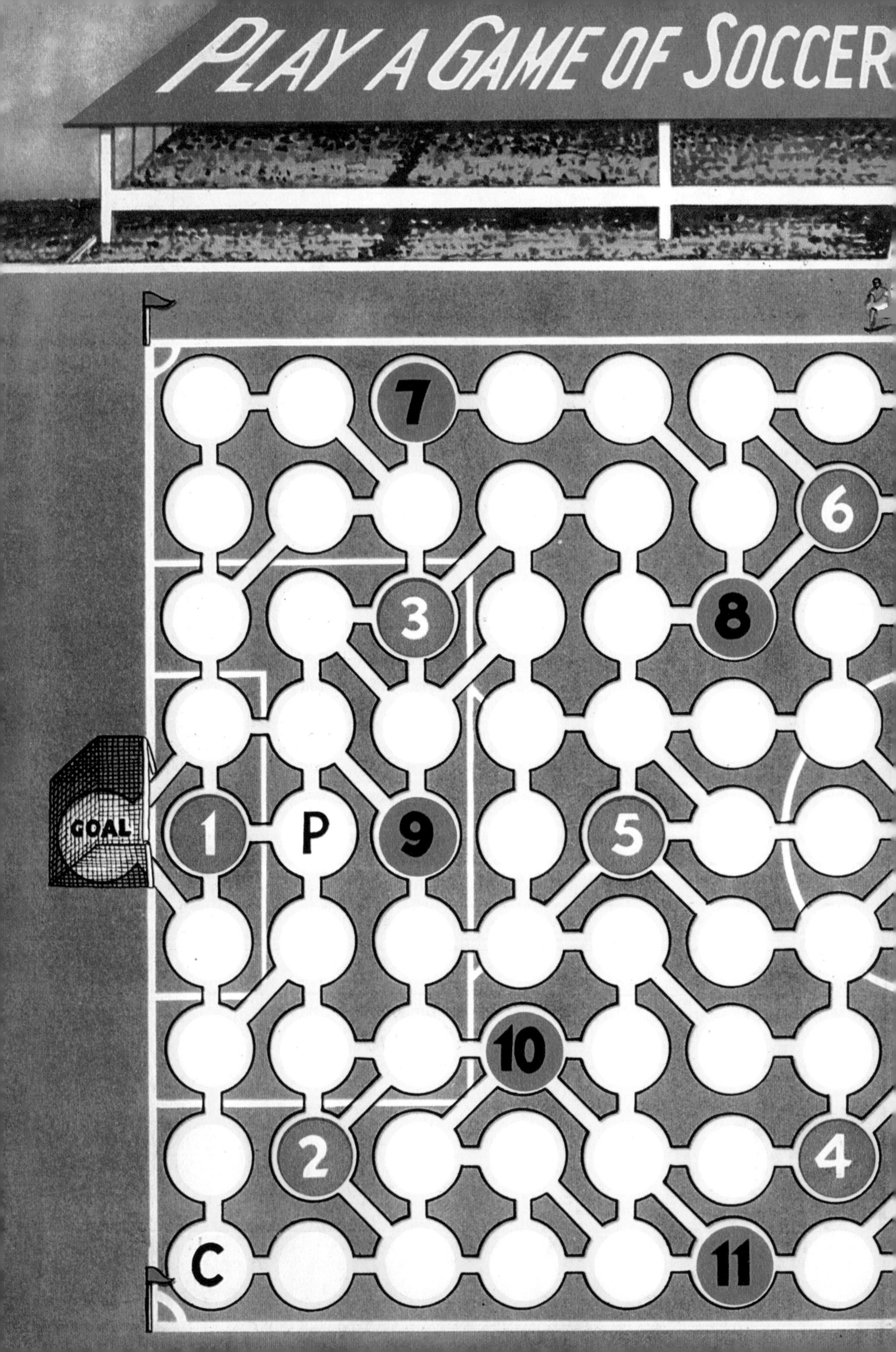
PLAY A GAME OF SOCCER
GOAL
7
6
3
8
1
P
9
5
10
2
4
C
11

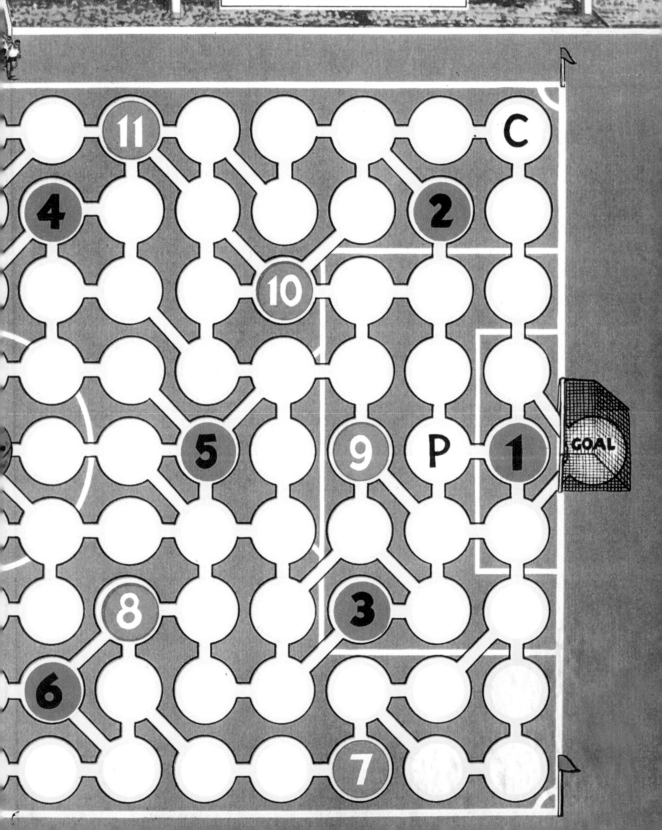

MELCHESTER STADIUM

HERE'S A THRILLING FOOTER GAME FOR TWO
PLAYERS.   YOU'LL NEED A DICE AND A SMALL
COIN FOR A BALL.   TURN TO PAGE 117 FOR THE
COMPLETE RULES.